# Attacks on the Press

Founded in 1981, the Committee to Protect Journalists responds to attacks on the press worldwide. CPJ documents hundreds of cases every year and takes action on behalf of journalists and news organizations without regard to political ideology. To maintain its independence, CPJ accepts no government funding. CPJ is funded entirely by private contributions from individuals, foundations, and corporations.

# Attacks on the Press

## 2014 EDITION

## *Journalism on the World's Front Lines*

### Committee to Protect Journalists

WILEY | **Bloomberg** PRESS

Cover photo: A journalist with Uganda's *The Independent* magazine faces off with police at a May 2013 protest over the closure of local news outlets including *The Daily Monitor, Kfm,* and *Red Pepper.* (Edward Echwalu)
Cover design: John Emerson

Editorial Director: Elana Beiser
Special Projects Editor: Larry Heinzerling
Deputy Editors: Shazdeh Omari, Kamal Singh Masuta
Copy Editor: Lew Serviss

*Library of Congress Cataloging-in-Publication Data:*

ISBN 978-1-118-87311-3 (Paperback)
ISBN 978-1-118-87307-6 (ePDF)
ISBN 978-1-118-87308-3 (ePub)

Printed in the United States of America
10  9  8  7  6  5  4  3  2  1

MIX
Paper from
responsible sources
FSC® C005928

# Contents

Contents

## 5. Controlling the Narrative

## 6. Legacies on the Line

# Foreword

## *By Jacob Weisberg*

In the midst of the Edward Snowden disclosures about the U.S. National Security Agency's electronic surveillance and data-mining programs, Gen. Keith Alexander sat down for a video interview with an in-house blogger at the Defense Department. "I think it's wrong that newspaper reporters have all these documents, the 50,000—whatever they have—and are selling them and giving them out . . ." the director of the National Security Agency said. "We ought to come up with a way of stopping it. I don't know how to do that. That's more of the courts and the policymakers but, from my perspective, it's wrong to allow this to go on."

The part about journalists selling documents was casual slander, or possibly just a cliché, if Alexander's point was that the press exploits news to sell newspapers. But his belief that the press should be prevented from reporting classified information represents something altogether more pernicious. This position, which some may recognize as the resurrected Nixon line in the Pentagon Papers case, has been in ascendance in the United States since the scandal at Iraq's Abu Ghraib prison in 2004. It has become a full-scale effort on the part of the U.S. and U.K. governments, and in the past year has emerged as the most significant threat to the free press in those countries.

One can understand the general's frustration, of course. Between WikiLeaks and Snowden, the security establishment has been doing a spectacularly poor job of keeping its secrets. This porousness may be intrinsic to the scale of the national surveillance state that has grown up since 9/11. More than 1.4 million people have "top secret" security clearances, 483,000 of them private contractors, with the provision of clearances itself now a profitable, privatized business. Like Snowden, many of the security-cleared find themselves collaborating in policies they come to regard as foolish, unethical, or simply wrongly hidden from public view. But the growing flow of leaks doesn't prompt Alexander and his colleagues to recognize that the scale of government secrecy is unworkable. It leads them to regard reporting on issues of security and surveillance as theft or treason. This is a conclusion that fundamentally misunderstands the role of journalism in a free society.

The proper rejoinder to Alexander's view is not that government should have no secrets, that Edward Snowden is a hero, or that leaking by a government official is never a criminal act. It is simply that in a democracy, the public has a right to know what the government is doing on its behalf. It is hard to imagine a place where that right becomes more fundamental than around the limits on tracking our words, thoughts, and communications. Technology makes the problem of unchecked government power more complex in practice; America's founding fathers could not have anticipated Britain's Government Communications Headquarters teaming with the NSA to tap into undersea fiber-optic cables in order to access email backed up at Google's data centers. It should not make it any different in theory. You can argue that the NSA should have the right to do what it has been doing. You cannot plausibly argue that it has the right to operate without democratic consent, genuine congressional supervision, or clear legal authority.

With clandestine operations comes the near-certainty of overreach and abuse. Former President Harry Truman opposed the creation of the CIA because he feared it would turn into an American Gestapo. Some president should have worried a little more about the NSA turning into an American Stasi. The NSA's inspector-general has acknowledged a dozen incidents of employees tracking the phone calls and emails of former girlfriends, subjects of romantic rather than legal interest, and in one case an "unfaithful husband." Further up the chain, they were listening in on the cellphone conversations of German Chancellor Angela Merkel. In the words of the historian and journalist Anne Applebaum, "The United States collects information because it can, whether or not it is moral to do so, violates the trust of allies, or is a monumental waste of time and money."

When the press asserts the need for public accountability, it is invariably accused of helping the bad guys. If one posits a stupid enough terrorist, this becomes an argument against ever reporting anything: Those who do not know that phones can be tapped are more likely to give themselves away if you do not go out of the way to tell them. In the real world, terrorists already know we are listening. That is why Osama bin Laden lived in a bunker that emitted no electronic signals. Making plain our intelligence capabilities is arguably an effective defensive measure. When terrorists are forced to avoid all electronic communication, their ability to plan attacks across borders is drastically curtailed. To be sure, the possible consequences of exposing secrets cannot always be predicted or controlled. But it is worth pointing out that in historical terms, the downside of public disclosure has been very small, while the cost of excessive secrecy has been enormous.

The British and American press has been tremendously scrupulous about the risk of endangering individuals and compromising operations. Perhaps too scrupulous—Margaret Sullivan, the public editor of the *New York Times*, has concluded that the paper should not have bowed to the Bush Administration in withholding its first revelations about extra-legal NSA wiretapping until after the 2004 election. The American Civil Liberties Union argues that the *Washington Post* has withheld too much technical detail about how the NSA accesses data from phone and Internet companies. If editors sometimes err on the side of caution, it is because they understand the need to weigh the risks of revelation against the damage of keeping citizens in the dark.

Despite the seriousness with which the press takes this responsibility, any reporter who works on these issues will tell you that he works in growing peril. In a special CPJ report, former *Washington Post* executive editor Leonard Downie, Jr., writes, "The administration's war on leaks and other efforts to control information are the most aggressive I've seen since the Nixon administration." In the past year alone, the Obama Justice Department secretly seized two months' worth of the Associated Press's phone records to track down a leak from the CIA; it labeled Fox News reporter James Rosen a co-conspirator in a State Department leak investigation and subpoenaed the phone records of his parents in Staten Island; it has vigorously appealed a federal court decision that *New York Times* reporter James Risen did not have to reveal a source in another leak case. This administration has charged more people under the 1917 Espionage Act, whose vagueness makes it easy for prosecutors to conflate whistle-blowing with treason, than all previous administrations combined.

Of course, the U.S. remains one of the safest countries in which to report on national security issues. Worldwide, dozens of journalists are jailed on anti-state charges and reporters are particularly vulnerable in Turkey, Iran, China, and Vietnam. But now throughout the free world, the dragnet of electronic surveillance is forcing journalists who work on security issues to conduct their trade like money launderers or drug dealers, encrypting their emails and communicating with sources on untraceable "burner" phones. A particular chill has descended in the U.K., where Alan Rusbridger and the *Guardian* have courageously driven the WikiLeaks and Snowden stories without the protections of a First Amendment or a written Constitution. In July, government officials arrived at the paper's offices to oversee the physical destruction of hard drives containing the Snowden material.

It is not just Gen. Alexander who thinks there ought to be a law against the press letting the public know who might be watching and listening. One of the more discouraging spectacles of the past year has been the way some elements of the popular press in the U.K. have called for their own colleagues to be prosecuted under the Official Secrets Act or the Terrorism Act. The *Daily Mail* calls the *Guardian* "the paper that helps Britain's enemies." Even as Barton Gellman of the *Washington Post* was breaking the Snowden news, his own paper's editorial board was calling for the leaks to be stopped. Journalists must hang together in holding our metastasizing surveillance states accountable. If not, we shall all hang separately.

*Jacob Weisberg is chairman of the Slate Group. He is the author of several books, including* The Bush Tragedy, *and is a member of CPJ's board of directors.*

# 1

# UNDER SURVEILLANCE

# How United States' Spying Strengthens China's Hand

*By Joel Simon*

**Demonstrators march outside of the U.S. Capitol in Washington on October 26, 2013, to demand that Congress investigate the NSA's mass surveillance programs.**

*Source:* AP/Jose Luis Magana.

In its typically fulminating style, the English language edition of China's *People's Daily* proclaimed in an August 2012 editorial that the U.S. must cede control of the Internet. "The Internet has become one of the most important resources in the world in just a few decades, but the governance mechanism for such an important international resource is still dominated by a private sector organization and a single country," the newspaper noted.

China is not alone in this view. A coalition of Internet-restricting nations—including Russia, Iran, Saudi Arabia, and countries throughout Africa and the Middle East—have formed an international coalition calling for the United Nations to take over Internet governance.

The Chinese argument that the Internet structure serves U.S. "hegemonic interests" was long viewed by the international community as "cynical and hypocritical," said Dan Gilmor, an author and expert on Internet issues, given the fact that U.S. policy has supported and promoted freedom of expression online while China has built a massive and sophisticated system of Internet control.

But the ever-growing revelations about the scope of digital spying carried out by the National Security Agency raise doubts about the U.S. commitment. The documents leaked by former NSA contractor Edward Snowden show that some of the U.S. spying programs operated with technical support of technology companies subject to U.S. jurisdiction. The NSA took advantage of the fact that nearly all online communications passes through U.S.-based servers and switches to vacuum up a huge portion of global communication. It specifically targeted governments, including allies like Brazil, whose president, Dilma Rousseff, has taken grave offense at the invasion of her personal correspondence.

By using its technological advantage and indirect control over the Internet to carry out a global surveillance operation of unprecedented scale, Gilmor told The Committee to Project Journalists (CPJ), "The U.S. has abused its position, handing repressive regimes a lot of ammunition to be clamping down even more."

China has long argued that the United Nations–administered International Telecommunication Union (ITU) should assume the authority for setting technical standards that currently reside with ICANN, a quasi-private entity based in Los Angeles that operates under license from the U.S. Commerce Department. The *People's Daily* editorial was intended to set the stage for the latest meeting of the ITU, which took place in Dubai, United Arab Emirates, in December 2012. At that meeting, a coalition of African and Middle Eastern countries introduced a treaty to bring Internet governance under ITU control.

The U.S. and European nations worked feverishly against the proposal, and in the end more than 50 countries, including all eligible members of the EU, refused to sign. But subsequently the U.S./ EU coalition has been deeply strained by the Snowden revelations. Europeans, who place a much higher value on privacy, were outraged to learn that their personal data might have been accessed by the NSA. European leaders reacted with fury at the scope of the surveillance, with German officials calling the spying "reminiscent of the Cold War" and the French Foreign Ministry summoning the U.S. ambassador to offer a formal rebuke.

"The credibility of the United States as a global champion for freedom of expression and human rights is undoubtedly damaged by the NSA revelations," Marietje Schaake, a member of the European Parliament and leader on Internet freedom issues, told CPJ.

The decentralized nature of the Internet, which makes censorship or control much harder, is a great strength for journalists and others committed to the free flow of information and ideas. But if you believe, as China does, that national sovereignty trumps the individual right to freedom of expression, then the Internet's current structure not only undermines state authority but also imposes U.S. standards of freedom of expression on the entire world.

This was the argument that played out at the U.N. General Assembly in September 2012 in the aftermath of the *Innocence of Muslims* video. After President Obama called censorship "obsolete" and described freedom of expression as a "universal ideal," then–Egyptian President Mohamed Morsi pushed back, declaring that Egypt does not respect freedom of expression "that targets a specific religion or a specific culture." His views were echoed by other leaders.

The embrace by former Secretary of State Hillary Clinton of the "right to connect" during a landmark speech at the Newseum in January 2010 was initially hailed by online freedom advocates as a positive step. But in the aftermath of the NSA scandal, it looks less enlightened. Many governments are skeptical of U.S. support for online freedom and believe that the U.S. commitment to free expression and association online is really about using the Internet to execute "regime change" and install client governments favorable to U.S. interests.

Iran under its last president, Mahmoud Ahmadinejad, announced plans to build a separate "halal" Internet closed off from the World Wide Web. In March 2012, Russian Duma member Aleksey Mitrofanov, head of the Parliamentary Committee on Information Policy, announced legislation to curtail online speech. "An era of absolutely free Internet in Russia has ended," he declared. Since then, courts have shut down critical websites—one Internet news site was stripped of its license for posting videos containing "foul language"— and the country's leading blogger, Aleksei Navalny, was convicted of trumped-up bribery charges.

Using powerful computers and technical acumen, the NSA has cracked encryption codes, making it possible for the U.S. government to gain access to nearly anything that moves online, according to a report by ProPublica. This has given the U.S. a tremendous strategic advantage, since it is widely believed to be the only country in the world with this capability. While the scope of online spying is still unfolding, the U.S. has hacked into the internal communication of at least one media outlet, according to a report in *Der Spiegel*. Citing leaked Snowden documents, the German magazine reported that the U.S. accessed Al-Jazeera's internal communications in 2006.

Both Germany and Brazil have indicated they will assert greater control over their domestic Internet. Deutsche Telekom, which is partially government-owned, is seeking an alliance with other German Internet providers to shield the German network from foreign snooping. The Brazilian Congress, meanwhile, is considering legislation that would require Internet companies operating in the country to store their data on domestic servers, a proposal opposed by international communications and technology companies, which say such a system would be prohibitively expensive.

Brazil is also advocating a new U.N. treaty to safeguard privacy. Speaking at the U.N. General Assembly in September 2013, President Rousseff said Brazil would "present proposals for the establishment of a civilian multi-lateral framework for the governance and use of the Internet and to ensure the effective protection of data that travels through it." Eduardo Bertoni, who directs a global freedom of expression center at the University of Palermo in Buenos Aires, Argentina, called on Brazil to "take concrete actions in support of Rousseff's words" including disavowing the ITU treaty, which Brazil signed.

Internationalizing Internet governance is, of course, not inherently a bad thing. In fact, proponents of the current "multi-stakeholder model" of Internet governance are also calling for a reduced U.S. role. At an October 2013 conference in Montevideo, Uruguay, the leaders of the organizations that coordinate the Internet's technical structure called for the "globalization" of ICANN functions. The signatories included the head of ICANN, Fadi Chehadé.

Rebecca MacKinnon, author of a book about online free expression called *Consent of the Networked* and a CPJ board member, pointed out that the multi-stakeholder model, in which constituencies including governments, companies, and civil society groups share responsibility for Internet governance, is flawed but "better than going to the U.N."

She added: "The role that the United States has been trying to preserve as a protector of freedom of openness—not too many people take it seriously any more. If we want to preserve the multi-holder model, then U.S. power needs to be reduced."

Schaake of the European Parliament agreed. "The negative impact of the exposure of the NSA activities is not limited to the United States' foreign policy objectives but could also harm the global open Internet, including the multi-stakeholder model as governments seek to take further control," she said. "We must ensure human rights and democratic principles are defended online. It is very worrying that the United States has undermined its own credibility to push these efforts." There is a risk in the current environment that an open debate will simply provide an enhanced platform for Internet-restricting countries like China to push for U.N. control. Success, while unlikely, would be a catastrophic event, according to MacKinnon, and would mean the end of the Internet as a shared global resource. "Around the world, countries are increasingly restricting the Internet and seeking to bring it under state control," Gilmor noted. He said he hoped the Snowden revelations "don't accelerate the trend, but I fear that they might."

■ ■ ■

Though the Chinese government argues that the free circulation of information across borders threatens its sovereign interests, it has no philosophical objection to using the Internet as a tool for surveillance. Beijing's primary complaint is that when it comes to Internet snooping, the U.S. has an unfair advantage.

During a meeting that CPJ hosted in September 2011 that brought together frontline journalists, technologists, and thought leaders from Silicon Valley, I was struck by the casual comment of a highly informed participant who claimed that the NSA loved encryption because the American agency can crack it and the Chinese can't. This view seems to have been confirmed by the Snowden revelations. The fact that the U.S. State Department has provided training for activists from around the world in the use of secure communication tools, including encryption and proxy servers that we know the NSA was able to monitor, looks cynical indeed—not least from the perspective of the Chinese or Iranian governments.

The massive state-sponsored Chinese hacking operation that targeted U.S. government agencies, the personal accounts of activists, and international media outlets including *The New York Times*, *The Wall Street Journal*, and Bloomberg prompted outrage and indignation from international press freedom organizations, including CPJ.

Though there is a real difference between the specific, targeted efforts to spy on international journalists carried out by Chinese authorities and the reputed use of metadata by the NSA to analyze patterns of communication, the Chinese hacking operation looks less aberrant today and more like an effort to level the playing field. The NSA spying operation has not only undercut U.S. moral authority, but has also made it more difficult for the international community to argue that the Chinese hacking operation falls outside international norms. After all, Google, which claimed it pulled out of China partly because Chinese hackers (by implication, with government sponsorship) targeted the personal emails of activists, provided information about its users to the U.S. government in order to comply with secret subpoenas.

Fearful of the U.S. snooping, countries are likely to look for alternatives to U.S. companies where possible. While Google and Facebook are the most popular sites in much of the world, according to a study by the Oxford Internet Institute, the search engine Baidu, which is partially state-owned, is dominant in China. "That means the NSA has much less reach into China at least via U.S. companies," MacKinnon pointed out. "China can say, 'Hey, from a national security perspective, we made the right call.'"

The global information ecosystem on which international journalism depends requires an open Internet that transcends borders. Global media organizations deliver the mass audience, but the reporting and information-sharing is now a networked phenomenon, with eyewitnesses to events using social media and other electronic means to communicate directly and indirectly with journalists who contribute their information and perspectives. The system clearly threatens autocratic regimes whose power depends on their ability to control information at least within their own borders.

Those governments have increased their technical ability to control and monitor communication over the past half decade. But their actions, for the most part, lacked international legitimacy. The unprecedented global spying operation carried out by the NSA has reduced the stigma. As a result, international journalists may see their global information networks disrupted in coming years as countries around the world step up their efforts to censor and monitor online communication. Already, some media organizations have changed the way they do business, including the *Guardian*. "You can no longer guarantee anonymity to a source," said Janine Gibson, who edited the groundbreaking stories by then–*Guardian* columnist Glenn Greenwald based on the Snowden leaks. "That's a terrifying thing for the journalists we work with."

*Joel Simon is the executive director of the Committee to Protect Journalists. His book,* Controlling the News, *will be published by Columbia University Press in 2014.*

# The NSA Puts Journalists Under a Cloud of Suspicion

*By Geoffrey King*

**The U.S. National Security Agency's data center in Bluffdale, Utah, has at least 100,000 square feet of the most advanced data reservoirs.**

*Source:* Reuters.

In fall 2013, the U.S. National Security Agency quietly began booting up its Utah Data Center, a sprawling 1.5 million-square-foot facility designed to store and analyze the vast amounts of electronic data the spy agency gathers from around the globe. Consisting of four low-slung data halls and a constellation of supporting structures, the facility includes at least 100,000 square feet of the most advanced data reservoirs in the world. The project represents a massive expansion of the NSA's capabilities and a profound threat to press freedom worldwide.

The data center is but the most obvious example of a future in which governments may not only collect and parse enormous quantities of data, but also store it for increasingly longer periods of time. The retention of surveillance data poses a unique threat to journalism in the digital age, particularly as technological advances allow the NSA and other intelligence agencies to store indefinitely not only the transactional details of all communications—as many experts believe is already the case—but also huge amounts of the content of phone calls, texts, and emails. By keeping a record of all communications transactions swept up in its dragnet, and then linking those transactions to content, the U.S. government could recreate a reporter's research, retrace a source's movements, and even retroactively listen in on communications that would otherwise have evaporated forever. It could soon be possible to uncover sources with such ease as to render meaningless any promise of confidentiality a journalist may attempt to provide—and if an interaction escapes scrutiny in the first instance, it could be reconstructed later.

Surveillance and persistent data storage have the potential to disrupt the free flow of information even in nations such as the U.S., which boasts strong protections for the freedom of the press. Journalists and sources alike will know that any story that draws official ire could be as likely to lead to exposure as to provoke public debate and reform. As long-term storage rapidly becomes less expensive, it will fall within the grasp of authoritarian regimes whose track records on press freedom afford little hope for restraint.

In addition to amplifying the harms caused by pervasive surveillance, the storage of data creates another, unique potential: It provides a deep breeding ground for artificial intelligence systems, which may in the future lead to more efficient, even predictive, spying machines.

As these capabilities evolve, governments will be able to spot patterns of terrorist activity, or journalistic activity, long before either becomes a challenge to their power. If left unchecked, surveillance systems may fail to draw such distinctions.

■ ■ ■

The NSA is infamously opaque, and many claims about it are impossible to confirm. Even the two main buildings at the agency's Fort Meade, Md., headquarters—named OPS2A and OPS2B—are literal black boxes of darkened, one-way glass. More significant than any physical obfuscation is the NSA's reticence about its operations: It is a well-known joke among agency insiders that the NSA's initials stand for "Never Say Anything" and "No Such Agency." Given such secretiveness, reporting on the agency often becomes an exercise in careful conjecture. Leaked documents from former NSA contractor Edward Snowden have shed some light on the agency's activities. For this report, CPJ interviewed veteran national security reporters, a lawyer challenging the constitutionality of the NSA's surveillance, and William Binney, who was considered one of the best mathematicians and code breakers at the NSA during his 30 years with the agency.

The experts with whom CPJ spoke all said they believe that the NSA targets journalists for surveillance. They disagreed about whether certain journalists are under more threat than others.

Binney, who resigned from the NSA in 2001 in protest of the mass privacy violations he alleges the agency committed after the 9/11 attacks, believes that the government keeps tabs on all reporters. He told CPJ, "They have a record of all of them, so they can investigate, so they can look at who they're calling—who are the potential sources that they're involved in, what probable stories they're working on, and things like that." Journalists, Binney noted, are "a much easier, smaller target set" to spy on than the wider population, and in his view, the NSA most likely takes advantage of this.

In contrast, national security journalist James Bamford, whom *The New Yorker* dubbed "The NSA's Chief Chronicler," told CPJ that he believes certain journalists get extra scrutiny. "If you're writing about national security or the NSA itself," he said, "they consider you—a journalist—a national security danger, and so they feel justified in doing whatever they're doing."

Alex Abdo, an American Civil Liberties Union attorney, is part of a team of lawyers who have litigated against the NSA for violating the privacy and free speech rights enshrined in the U.S. Constitution. He told CPJ that he believes that "all reporters should be worried," though perhaps for different reasons. "Reporters who work for the largest media organizations should be worried probably primarily because their sources will dry up as those sources recognize that there is no way to cover their trail" when they talk to journalists at *The New York Times*, *The Washington Post*, or *The Wall Street Journal*. For independent journalists, by contrast, the primary concern is that "they themselves will be swept up in the course of their reporting, because they don't enjoy some of the institutional protections that journalists get when they work at the bigger organizations."

Asked about surveillance of journalists, the NSA asserted that the primary function of its data collection is to protect the U.S. from foreign threats. Spokeswoman Vanee' Vines, herself a former investigative journalist, told CPJ, "NSA is focused on discovering and developing intelligence about *valid foreign intelligence targets* in order to protect the nation and its interests from threats such as terrorism and the proliferation of weapons of mass destruction." Vines also pointed to a statement on the NSA's Tumblr site that states, "NSA conducts all of its activities in accordance with applicable laws, regulations, and policies—and assertions to the contrary do a grave disservice to the nation, its allies and partners, and the men and women who make up the National Security Agency." (Intelligence officials have in the past misled the public about the NSA's activities. At a March 2013 Senate Intelligence Committee hearing, Sen. Ron Wyden asked Director of National Intelligence James Clapper, "Does the NSA collect any type of data at all on millions or hundreds of millions of Americans?" Clapper said, "No sir . . . not wittingly." After Snowden's revelations about the mass collection of Americans' phone call records, and facing accusations of perjury from members of Congress, Clapper sent a letter to the committee chairwoman, Sen. Dianne Feinstein, apologizing for his "clearly erroneous" remarks under oath.)

Russ Tice, who spent nearly 20 years working in various government agencies, claims to have firsthand knowledge of the targeting of journalists for surveillance. Speaking to Keith Olbermann in 2009, Tice alleged that, while an analyst at the NSA, he witnessed an agency program that gathered information on U.S. news organizations and journalists. He did not elaborate. And the NSA may not be the only U.S. intelligence agency monitoring journalists. In 2008, retired Army Sgt. Adrienne Kinne told *Democracy Now!*'s Amy Goodman and other journalists that, while in military intelligence, she listened to telephone conversations between journalists in Iraq and their spouses and editors, even though, as their identities became clear, their numbers could have been excluded from interception.

In addition to these allegations, in August 2013 the German magazine *Der Spiegel* reported that it had reviewed NSA documents, provided by Snowden, showing that the agency hacked into a "specially protected" internal communication system at the Qatar-based broadcaster Al-Jazeera. According to *Der Spiegel*, the NSA documents listed the operation as "a notable success." The NSA has not publicly commented on the report.

One journalist for whom surveillance apparently has had direct and recent consequences is the award-winning documentary filmmaker Laura Poitras, whose films showcase American policy in the post-9/11 era and who, with Glenn Greenwald, documented Snowden's revelations about the NSA in the *Guardian*. Poitras says she was detained for questioning at U.S. border crossings more than 40 times between 2006 and 2012; Snowden told Peter Maass for *The New York Times Magazine* that, because of her previous reporting, Poitras was "specifically becoming targeted by the very programs involved in the recent disclosures."

Comments by the head of the NSA, Gen. Keith Alexander, in October 2013, suggested that the agency has little patience for journalists who dig into its activities. "I think it's wrong that newspaper reporters have all these documents, 50,000 or whatever they have, and are selling them and giving them out as if these—you know it just doesn't make sense," he told the Defense Department's "Armed with Science" blog, as reported by *Politico*. "We ought to come up with a way of stopping it. I don't know how to do that, that's more of the courts and the policy makers, but from my perspective it's wrong, and to allow this to go on is wrong."

Most journalists will probably not end up in the NSA's cross-hairs. But all journalists need to recognize that the agency is collecting immense amounts of information, that it will continue to develop this capacity, and that once collected, this information can be retained and put to broad use. Thus, while a small-town reporter who writes about the state fair may not be as likely to be surveilled as a big-city national security reporter who writes about the affairs of nation-states, both are vulnerable—especially when surveillance data is indexed and stored.

■ ■ ■

Behind the Utah Data Center's battleship-gray walls sit the devices that make up what NSA Chief Information Officer Lonny Anderson has described as the NSA's "cloud." Although expert opinions regarding the facility's storage capacity vary widely, even the most conservative estimates are astounding. On the low end, it is thought that the Utah Data Center can store between 3 and 12 exabytes of data. (An exabyte is the equivalent of a billion gigabytes.) To put this in perspective, in 2003 researchers at the University of California, Berkeley, estimated that the amount of information generated by all conversations since the dawn of humanity would total about 5 exabytes. Bolder theorists such as the former NSA analyst Binney say the Utah facility will have a gross storage capacity of about one zettabyte, or 1,024 exabytes.

Binney told CPJ that the NSA is mapping individuals' lives, particularly their social and business connections, via the trail of digital "metadata" attendant with day-to-day existence. Though generally considered to exclude the contents of communications, and often transactional or descriptive in nature, metadata can be exquisitely detailed, as illustrated by a top secret order from the secretive U.S. Foreign Intelligence Surveillance Court (known as the FISA court) leaked to *The Guardian* by Snowden. According to the order, the NSA collects the numbers, location data, unique identifying information, and the time and duration of phone calls, for all parties. As reported by *The New York Times*, the FISA court has also authorized and reauthorized the collection and analysis of all Americans' call records, regardless of any connection to a foreign agent.

Although it is impossible to know of everything the NSA is collecting, courts have ruled in other contexts that information often considered to be metadata is not limited to phone calls and can include banking, Internet, email, and other records. Though judicial attitudes toward the privacy implications of metadata surveillance may slowly be shifting, as judges have begun to recognize its power to open up the lives of individuals to scrutiny, at present such data remains largely unprotected by the U.S. Fourth Amendment—meaning that even American journalists lack a so-called "reasonable expectation of privacy" for large amounts of their information.

The information gleaned from the aggregation of metadata records can build a remarkably intimate picture of one's life. As computer security expert Bruce Schneier wrote on his blog in September 2013, metadata analysis is the equivalent of hiring a private detective to keep tabs on a person's activities and associations. "The result would be details of what he did: where he went, who he talked to, what he looked at, what he purchased—how he spent his day," Schneier wrote. "That's all metadata."

Metadata surveillance is particularly dangerous to journalists because it means the government can quickly pinpoint their sources. Bamford said, "It's always dangerous when the government has access to journalists' communication because what journalists guarantee sources is confidentiality, and if there's no such thing as confidentiality from the government, it would inhibit the future cooperation from sources." This has a "very serious effect" on investigative journalism, he told CPJ. "If they're able to see all the numbers you're calling, they're able to tell pretty much what kind of story you're working on, even without getting the content of it. They're able to tell what the nature of the story is, who the sources are you're dealing with."

Metadata has an exceptionally small digital footprint that belies its intrusiveness. According to Binney, "You could build a graph for phones and emails and banking and carry the aggregate metadata graph of those domains and keep all that information in the size of a room 12 foot by 20 foot. And do it for the world, and keep it indexed for as many years as you want." (A January 2011 NSA memorandum obtained by *The New York Times* confirms the existence of such large-scale graph analysis.)

Given this technical reality, Binney said, it is clear that the NSA did not build its Utah facility for transactional data alone. When asked why the agency might need the kind of space it had constructed, Binney said: "It means content of communications, not just metadata. They are building more and more storage because they're collecting more and more." He said the NSA will "take everything" off communication lines "and store it" for perhaps half a million to a million targeted individuals. According to Binney, the content information will then be indexed to the graph of lives and social networks. The agency can then query a timeline of an individual's relationships over a period of time and "go straight into the content" indexed to each event. Binney's estimate is that the NSA has both content and metadata going back a dozen years, and that this will only grow over time.

The extent to which the NSA may lawfully gather, store, and disseminate the contents of communications about U.S. persons is more closely constrained by the Fourth Amendment, as well as by statutes such as the 2008 FISA Amendments Act and other regulations, than is metadata. Nonetheless, there are numerous ways for the NSA to harvest the contents of communications of American journalists. *The New York Times* reported in August 2013 that the NSA is copying and searching the contents of large amounts of Americans' cross-border communications, for the purpose of uncovering even mentions of small details—an email address, for example, or a nickname—about a foreigner under surveillance.

Additionally, under current regulations, incidentally-acquired communications of Americans can be retained for up to six years to analyze whether they contain foreign intelligence information and/or evidence of a crime, according to recently declassified documents and reporting by *The Washington Post* and *The Guardian*. This is true even for communications that turn out to have been purely domestic in nature. (According to *The New York Times*, a 2010 internal briefing paper from the NSA Office of Legal Counsel indicated that the agency was allowed to collect and store raw communications traffic from U.S. citizens and residents, including both metadata and content, for up to five years online and for 10 years for "historical searches." Encrypted communications may be kept indefinitely, documents leaked to the *Guardian* reveal.) According to a report by the Brennan Center for

Justice at NYU School of Law, the NSA can also share reports based on Americans' incidentally-acquired foreign communications—and under certain circumstances, the "unminimized communications" themselves—with the Central Intelligence Agency, the Federal Bureau of Investigation, and even foreign governments. Additionally, information about Americans' incidentally-acquired domestic communications may be shared with the FBI.

Though the amount of content stored subsequent to such collection cannot be established with certainty, some information came to light in the wake of the April 2013 Boston Marathon bombings that could prove instructive regarding the scope of content-based surveillance of U.S. citizens and residents. In an interview with CNN, former FBI counterterrorism agent Tim Clemente implied that even domestic telephone calls are being recorded in bulk and can be reproduced as needed. "All of that stuff is being captured as we speak whether we know it or like it or not," he said, noting later that "there's a way to look at digital communications in the past" and that "no digital communication is secure."

Internet Archive founder Brewster Kahle, a proponent of one of the more cautious estimates about the Utah Data Center's storage capacity, posted a spreadsheet in June 2013 estimating that if the NSA did record and store all U.S. phone calls, both foreign and domestic, it would cost only $27 million per year to do so.

■ ■ ■

As the government stores more and more data, it will become next to impossible for journalists to keep sources confidential. "The problem is, the more data you get, the more capacity you have to see into somebody's life," Binney said. "And it gets a much finer grain of picture of your electronic life. So capturing that and being able to collect all that data and correlate it then makes that picture of you much clearer. And that's only getting better with storage."

These advances illustrate why the Utah Data Center's present capabilities are far from the end of the story for journalists either in the U.S. or abroad. As the NSA's director for Installations and Logistics, Harvey Davis, put it to *The Salt Lake Tribune*, "I always build everything expandable." And in addition to the Utah facility, the NSA stores data at facilities in Hawaii, Colorado, Texas, Georgia, and Maryland. It is also possible that the agency has developed secret custom hardware, proprietary data compression algorithms, or other efficiency-enhancing techniques that would expand the amount of raw data that can be saved.

The dangers are further compounded for non–U.S. journalists. "Anyone who's not an American citizen or not somebody within the United States—there are no protections at all," Bamford said. If a British, French, or German journalist were to undertake "an investigative story on something involving the U.S., some war crime committed by somebody in the U.S.," the NSA, he said, "can do whatever they want in terms of finding out who their sources are."

The ACLU's Abdo agrees. "Even a mainstream reporter abroad has a different type of worry than a mainstream reporter in the United States," he said. "I would be surprised, for example, if the U.K. office of the *Guardian* were not the subject of significant NSA surveillance." Abdo's comments follow the revelation from *Guardian* Editor Alan Rusbridger in August that security agents from Government Communications Headquarters—Britain's version of the NSA—oversaw the destruction of computer hard drives at the *Guardian* in a bid to prevent the newspaper from reporting further on Snowden's documents. (The *Guardian* rendered GCHQ's efforts futile by forging a partnership with *The New York Times* and the non-profit news group ProPublica, which as American organizations enjoy significant legal protections from prior restraint under the U.S. Constitution.)

Citing the Constitution, veteran reporter Peter Maass expressed defiance. "Does it worry me to know that the government can store stuff and recreate stuff, whereas in the past, it would need to have specific court orders in order to listen to and store my phone calls? Yeah," he told CPJ. "This is the reason why we're all writing these stories—and that we find problems in what the government is doing." Ultimately, Maass sees the NSA's activities as an opportunity for educating the public. "The more the government does this, the more they are creating a problem for themselves, and journalists like myself are going to go at it 110 percent, because they are such core constitutional challenges," he said. "Part of me says bring it on."

Maass recognizes, however, that just as the U.S. takes the gloves off when dealing with foreign journalists, other actors are likely to handle Americans the same way. "The NSA and the U.S. government are not the only threat" to the work of American journalists, he notes. "The Russian government is interested in it, and the British government is interested in it, private interests are interested in it," he said. "So we have to be aware of that."

Advances in technology could soon allow nearly any government to engage in unprecedented levels of surveillance and storage. According to a 2011 report by the Brookings Institution, data storage costs have declined by a factor of 10 roughly every four years over the past three decades. In 1984, a gigabyte of storage cost $85,000 in 2011 dollars; in 2011, a gigabyte cost 5 cents, according to the study. Based on these numbers, in 2011 it would have cost Syria—which in 2012–2013 was the fourth-highest exporter of journalists fleeing for their lives—only about $2.5 million to record all calls made by its citizens. By 2016 that number could drop to $250,000, and by 2020, to $25,000.

While the experts debate the fine points, working journalists are forced to examine their own practices. Ali Winston, an award-winning freelance investigative reporter based in the San Francisco Bay area, told CPJ that the dual threat of pervasive surveillance and data storage "has made me rethink my own privacy. It has made me conscious of how I treat my sources, and it has made me conscious that I don't want things to fall back on my sources."

Winston, who graduated from the UC Berkeley Graduate School of Journalism in 2010, said he has tried to mitigate the exploitation of his electronic communications for years, including by using the anonymizing software Tor, and has taken new security steps given recent revelations about surveillance. He cites as a turning point the 2005 revelation by James Risen and Eric Lichtblau in *The New York Times* of the NSA's initial warrantless wiretapping program. "I began to educate myself by reading James Bamford's books, by reading the newspaper, by reading the back stories," of surveillance initiatives, Winston told CPJ. "There is an innate logic in surveillance systems towards expansions," he said. "There are no natural checks on surveillance. They will continue to gather information until a block is put in front of it."

■ ■ ■

As dangerous as the NSA's expanding storage capabilities are to journalism, the trend carries an even darker prospect. The growth of data collection and storage provides a training ground for artificial intelligence systems designed to fish information efficiently from a vast sea of data. "It's basically a gold mine for those kind of processes," Binney told CPJ of the databases. "They need an automated algorithm to go through and figure out what is important." According to Binney, the ultimate goal is to be predictive. "They want to get to the point where they can be doing intentions and capabilities of potential threats," he said.

Bamford wrote about earlier data initiatives in his 2008 book, *The Shadow Factory*. These initiatives included a 2004 pilot project that used information taken from news articles to build a computerized brain capable of predicting events. As Bamford wrote, "Once up and running, the database of old newspapers could quickly be expanded to include an inland sea of personal information scooped up by the agency's warrantless data suction hoses. . . . Unregulated, they could ask it to determine which Americans might likely pose a security risk—or have sympathies toward a particular cause." As Bamford reported, the project, which was still going at least as late as 2009, was sufficiently troublesome that an unnamed researcher resigned over moral concerns.

If the NSA manages to develop a system that could automatically assign a threat index to members of the public, the agency would almost certainly use it to give journalists extra attention. Even journalists who do not find themselves under scrutiny for their work are at risk. As Cynthia Wong of Human Rights Watch noted in an analysis posted on the organization's website in August 2013, reporters are among the relatively few regular users of privacy-enhancing technologies. This alone, Bamford told CPJ, is enough for the government to target reporters. "I don't use encryption," he said. "No. 1, it flags you, and No. 2, it gives [the NSA] more of an incentive to try and break it." (At least one expert disagrees: Snowden told *The New York Times Magazine* that "unencrypted journalist-source communication is unforgivably reckless.")

By automating processes, the NSA is lowering the opportunity costs of surveillance. As profound as the possibilities may be, in the near term automation makes such processes both more intelligent and less. "You've got the NSA collecting everybody's phone records, so whenever you pick up the phone, there's a record with NSA," Bamford said. "You have machines that are making these connections, and they may have no rational basis." An individual who reaches out to a controversial source for information may end up paying for it later, he said. "All you're seeing is that there's a link between a target and a U.S. citizen, and now that U.S. citizen becomes a suspect."

Binney agrees. "Just because you call the pizza guy and I call the same pizza guy doesn't mean we have a relationship," he said. "So there's no reason to collapse us into that community, based on that one call to the pizza guy."

Said Bamford, "The NSA is gathering power and they're gathering more capabilities and more eavesdropping, more invasive technologies." He added, "At the same time, they're deceiving the very weak organizations that are supposed to be the oversight mechanisms—the Congress and the FISA Court. I think it's a very worrying situation, not just for journalists, but for anybody."

The revelations about surveillance have changed the way journalists must think about the security of their work product, their sources, and themselves. Prudent journalists wishing to avoid scrutiny for themselves or their sources will have to adapt their behavior, whether by avoiding contact with sources or ceasing to use privacy-protective technologies such as encryption. Such changes impair journalists' ability to freely gather and disseminate information.

Regardless of whether the NSA's programs are as carefully targeted as it claims, the agency's infamous secrecy and expansive capabilities have cast a deep shadow on press freedom worldwide. When even sophisticated digital self-help is merely an imperfect solution, the only true recourse is to force transparency through ever more incisive reporting, for as Supreme Court Justice Louis Brandeis wrote 100 years ago, "Sunlight is said to be the best of disinfectants."

*CPJ Internet Advocacy Coordinator **Geoffrey King** works to protect the digital rights of journalists worldwide. A constitutional lawyer by training, King, who is based in San Francisco, also teaches courses at UC Berkeley on digital privacy law and on the intersection of media and social change.*

# 2

# THE INFORMATION
# IMPERATIVE

# Putting Press Freedom at the Heart of Anti-Poverty Efforts

*By Robert Mahoney*

**Pakistani journalist Umar Cheema, right, accepts CPJ's International Press Freedom Award in 2011 from David Rohde of Reuters. Cheema has successfully uncovered corruption in his country but has few supporters.**

*Source:* Committee to Protect Journalists.

Umar Cheema, a Pakistani journalist, wrote often about the military. Then one night masked men hauled him from his car and during six hours of torture, sexual humiliation, and threats, they made it clear that the reporting should stop. Cheema not only refused to stop writing, he went public with his ordeal. "I wanted to send a message that I had not cowed down," Cheema said of his response to the 2010 assault. "I did nothing wrong, and that kept me strong." The Committee to Protect Journalists (CPJ) awarded him its International Press Freedom Award in 2011.

The assault spurred him on to do more reporting, and, in December 2012, he launched the Center for Investigative Reporting in Pakistan. To mark the opening, he published a list of members of Parliament who paid no taxes and ignited a political firestorm. Despite his success in unearthing wrongdoing and corruption—some might even say because of it—Cheema has few powerful domestic allies or financial backers to develop his work.

There are Umar Cheemas in most countries, ferreting out land titles, company accounts, and public records, in an effort to hold governments and businesses accountable and serve the public interest. But many are underfunded and exposed. They are harassed, or threatened, or lose their jobs. An increasing number are imprisoned, and many are simply murdered.

Their work and the broader role of journalists and media organizations as a voice for the poor and powerless, a provider of information and ideas, a forum for politics and culture, and an engine of change is acknowledged by economists and political scientists as vital to economic development and democracy.

But multilateral institutions from the United Nations to the World Bank, along with individual Western donor nations and agencies, have a mixed record in providing the sustained support, protection, and investment that journalists in repressive or impoverished countries or regions require.

At the dawn of this millennium, world leaders vowed to improve the health and welfare of much of humanity by 2015 and agreed on eight goals for doing so. Press freedom was not among them. Neither were democratic governance and accountability, which press freedom underpins.

The U.N.'s Millennium Development Goals are credited by some economists with helping mobilize support for overseas development aid, which rose sharply between 2001 and the financial crash of 2008. The increase contributed to lifting about 500 million people out of extreme poverty, although some economists argue that the economic rise of China was as much a factor in this success as a surge in aid.

Whatever their achievements, the eight goals have been overtaken, not least by the explosion in communication technology, and no longer fully address peoples' aspirations. According to the U.N.'s own poll of more than half a million people worldwide in 2013, citizens want the U.N. to focus on promoting open and responsive government, which they ranked as a priority behind only food and health care.

Keeping politicians, government officials, and business people honest, however, is no easy task, especially in poor countries where institutions, civil society and the rule of law are weak. The role of journalists and bloggers empowered by new technologies in helping to improve the lives of ordinary citizens has never been clearer, and the price that some of them pay in terms of their own lives or liberty has never been higher. International and regional institutions that promote economic development or security are increasingly aware of the role of journalists as defenders of human rights, vital to promoting transparent and accountable government.

This awareness surfaced in a U.N.–commissioned report by 27 prominent political leaders and experts that freedom of expression advocates welcomed as an opportunity to put press freedom on the U.N. agenda.

The Report of the High-Level Panel of Eminent Persons on the Post-2015 Development Agenda published in May 2013, lays out ways to end extreme poverty. The report, titled "A New Global Partnership: Eradicate Poverty and Transform Economies through Sustainable Development," has as one of its recommended goals the promotion of "good governance and effective institutions." To reach that goal the leaders identify two necessary conditions: "ensure that people enjoy freedom of speech, association, peaceful protest and access to independent media and information," and "guarantee the public's right to information and access to government data."

"This report is hugely welcome," writes James Deane, director of policy and learning at BBC Media Action, the BBC's international development charity. "It presents a fresh, ambitious agenda that provides a comprehensive framework for meeting a set of immense development challenges. It does so by putting issues of governance and rights—including freedom of the media—at its heart, not its periphery. That has not happened before."

The panel, which was headed by British Prime Minister David Cameron and Presidents Susilo Bambang Yudhoyono of Indonesia and Ellen Johnson Sirleaf of Liberia, also called for a "data revolution" for citizens to access information and statistics and for governments to make them available.

"I'm excited that we have expanded the boundaries," said the report's lead author, Homi Kharas of the Brookings Institution. "The press has an extremely important role to play . . . in holding authorities and private companies accountable," he told CPJ.

That a free press and democratic governance go hand in hand is now well established in the development community. But it was not always so, as made evident by the glaring omissions in the first set of U.N. goals in 2000.

The World Bank started considering press freedom in its assessments in the 1990s. "We showed that corruption mattered for economic development," said economist Daniel Kaufmann, president of the Revenue Watch Institute, who used to work at the World Bank in several capacities, including as lead economist.

However, over the years, a number of authoritarian countries have become uneasy with the bank's focus on governance. Kaufmann added that there has been "pushback" by economically powerful states unsympathetic to policies that promote press freedom and accountability, and that, he said, has made implementing a global policy difficult.

■ ■ ■

Reporters rely on institutional support to do the kinds of watchdog journalism that keep democracy healthy. These conditions include rule of law, functioning state institutions, an independent judiciary, access to information, and strong civil society groups.

Some of these elements were present in a few Eastern European countries, including Poland and the Czech Republic, in the years after the collapse of the Soviet Union, and press freedom and governance made important strides in both countries. After Indonesia shook off the yoke of President Suharto, the press played an important role in nudging the country toward greater democracy.

This was also true in post-apartheid South Africa. Since Nelson Mandela left office, however, some officials and business people have sought to cover up corruption or incompetence, and media groups and human rights activists have had to push back against threats of encroachment on free expression and access to information.

"Many newly free or newly democratic states celebrate freedom of the media, often because brave reporting helped them to become free," South African editor Brendan Boyle told CPJ. "But many of those same states and governments turn against the same reporters and media when the reality of transforming their societies starts to bite and the media report on their failings."

As editor of the *Daily Dispatch* in East London, Boyle had a pair of young reporters investigate corruption and mismanagement in South Africa's school hostels. Education is a prime sector of the Millennium Development Goals strategy. His reporters won the CNN Africa Journalist Award for 2013. "The reports led to some improvements but also saw the newspaper banned this month from covering the annual year-end examinations for school leavers," Boyle, who has since become executive editor of South Africa's *Sunday Times*, added.

For decades, authoritarian leaders of emerging economies have tried to promote "development journalism," that is, insisting journalists accentuate positive news in the name of economic advancement. This has become prevalent in Africa, where China's growing economic and political clout has spilled over to journalism. Autocrats from Gambia to Ethiopia laud their own versions of a Chinese media development model, arguing that critical or "socially irresponsible" journalism and pesky investigative reporting hurt the economy, undermine stability, and deter foreign investors. The Ugandan Parliament still has a bill before it that could criminalize reporting that the authorities deem "economic sabotage."

This false choice between development and press freedom has been pedaled by autocrats throughout much of the life of the millennium goals. The High-Level Panel's report explodes that argument by placing democratic governance at the core of any anti-poverty drive and recognizing the role of a free press in achieving it.

"Making media freedom a formal measure of good governance with potential links to the assessment of investment risk would not only help to protect reporters and publications but to protect societies from governments unable or unwilling to protect and to serve their people," Boyle said.

Challenging the economy-versus-rights narrative can be dangerous and underlines the need for a comprehensive international approach to defend journalists. The figures speak for themselves: More journalists were behind bars in 2012—some 232 worldwide—than at any time since CPJ began counting them in 1990. In the past 15 years, the trend line for journalists killed for their work has been rising, averaging more than 47 deaths per year.

Significantly, the ability or willingness of states to prosecute those who murder journalists and other advocates of civil liberties is lacking. CPJ's global Impunity Index shows that hundreds of murder cases involving journalists remain unprosecuted and that 26 percent of those killed were covering corruption. Threatened with harm, and unprotected by the authorities, many reporters have simply fled. The number of journalists in exile, whether from fear of persecution or imprisonment in Sri Lanka or Ethiopia, or fear of being killed in Syria or Somalia, is growing.

Despite some success stories in countries that have shaken off autocratic rule, the overall environment for critical journalism has not improved in recent years. Freedom House, the Washington foundation that promotes democracy, publishes a global press freedom index that, if averaged out, has flatlined since the mid-1990s. The percentage of countries that Freedom House deems free dropped to 35 from 39 in the decade after 2000.

"Essentially the past decade or more has been a decade lost in terms of media freedom around the world," said Kaufmann, the economist.

■ ■ ■

The reasons for the decline in press freedom and the rise in deaths and imprisonment of journalists are complex. It is an area that needs more rigorous academic analysis and better diagnostics, according to media development experts interviewed for this article.

Technology has enabled journalists and bloggers to self-publish, but authoritarian governments have quickly learned how to turn the same technology into a tool for censoring and tracking critical reporters. The cost of entry into the news business has been lowered to the point that anyone with a smartphone can be a reporter and publisher. This has dramatically increased the number of people who are able to report events, particularly in conflict zones and repressive environments, thereby increasing the number of reporters who get into trouble.

Journalists themselves and media development groups have pushed the United Nations to do more to protect reporters, starting in 2006 with the adoption of Security Council Resolution 1738, which underlined the civilian status of and protections due to reporters covering conflict. Since then, these groups have urged the U.N. to incorporate the protection of journalists into its broader work.

In May 2013, this bore fruit in the form of a U.N. Plan of Action on the Safety of Journalists and the Issue of Impunity. The plan calls for a new U.N. inter-agency mechanism to assess journalist safety, for greater powers for the U.N. special rapporteur on freedom of expression, and for assistance to member states in passing national legislation to prosecute the killers of journalists. It envisions partnerships between the U.N. and media safety groups along with global awareness campaigns. It also calls for development of emergency response procedures for journalists in the field and provisions for press safety in conflict zones.

But even this victory was hard won and shows the enormous obstacles that have to be overcome in a multinational body in which member states suspicious of an independent news media have influence. The adoption of the plan was in doubt for some time after Pakistan, India, and Brazil, all of which have long histories of high levels of violence against journalists, objected to certain provisions. After pressure from CPJ and others, Brazil relented and backed the plan.

Champions of freedom of expression are now girding for what will doubtless be a hard battle to shepherd the High-Level Panel's press freedom goal through the political wrangling of the U.N. and into the final framework. The panel's 12 goals and 54 related national targets are just one of several reports that will land on the desk of U.N. Secretary

General Ban Ki-moon by the end of 2014. He will synthesize them into one report, which will be the starting point for inter-governmental politicking that will culminate in a special September 2015 summit to agree on the final document.

"I don't want to be too simplistic but, on the issue of press freedom, countries that oppose press freedom in their own country are going to be our main spoilers on this agenda," a U.K. diplomat at the country's U.N. mission in New York who follows the issue told CPJ.

Jan Lublinski, a research and development manager at DW Akademie, a media development agency affiliated with the German broadcaster Deutsche Welle, agrees. "It will not be easy to convince authoritarian regimes to commit to such an agenda," he told CPJ.

Lublinski and his colleagues have already begun speculating on what form the framework could take. "It may be easier to define and agree upon a new set of development goals without explicit mention of freedom of expression, information rights and the media," they wrote in a discussion paper. "But such a choice would also mean avoiding an answer to the challenges the world faces today. A new MDG"—Millennium Development Goals—"agenda that focuses on poverty, health, environment, gender equality, and education only, would neglect essential elements of the human rights as well as governance processes with all their potential influence on other development sectors."

Kharas, the High-Level Panel report's lead author, thinks it's too early to speculate on the likely language of the final document. He suggests supporters not only argue for the effectiveness of press freedom as an instrument of economic development but also stress that freedom of expression is a basic human right as guaranteed by the U.N.'s own founding principles and enshrined in Article 19 of the Universal Declaration of Human Rights.

Guy Berger, director of UNESCO's freedom of expression unit, echoes the human rights argument. "If press freedom is not ultimately recognized in the 2015 agenda, it would be a missed opportunity for a human-rights centered, richly rounded and practically effective understanding of development," he told CPJ. "In fact, the recognition of the important role of free media in the report is much greater than that of the Internet and ICTs," he said, referring to information and communications technologies. "By treating development as a human, not technology-driven, process, the issue of rights is inseparable from the concept of development."

This point that press freedom is a basic human right sometimes gets lost in the diplomatic maneuvering and contortions over wording behind U.N. agreements, but it is one that journalists and their allies will need to make.

"This is the time for advocacy," the U.K. diplomat at the U.N. said. "I think that it is one of the more controversial components of this report and has absolutely no guarantee to get into the final framework. . . . If we want it in the final framework, we and other likeminded member states and civil society organizations are going to need to fight pretty forcefully for its inclusion."

Whatever document is eventually drafted in New York, reporters like Umar Cheema will continue to probe the dark corners of Pakistani society, often with minimal resources and protection from the state, because that's what reporters do.

"I still feel the power of truth, and it keeps me moving now. I try to be more and more objective, and when you are objective, half of your fear is gone," he said, knowing that many courageous journalists have been silenced in recent years—for good.

*Robert Mahoney is CPJ's deputy director. He has worked as a reporter, editor, and bureau chief for Reuters throughout the world. Mahoney has led CPJ missions to global hot spots from Iraq to Sri Lanka.*

# Without Stronger Transparency, More Financial Crises Loom

*By Michael J. Casey*

**Sharp swings in the stock market have led to questions about who stands to benefit from high-frequency trading.**

*Source:* AP/Richard Drew.

T
he social forces that can encourage euphoria among investors and then suddenly flip them into mass panic are not unlike those that generate crowd disasters such as the stampedes that have killed more than 2,500 pilgrims at Mecca since 1990.

In such moments of herd-like behavior, the common element is a profound lack of information. If neither the individuals in an enthusiastic crowd nor those charged with policing it have a grasp on how it is behaving as a whole, the mob can grow too big for its surroundings. Equally, if those people are ill-informed about the extent of the risks they face when they discover something is wrong, they will assume the worst and rush for the exits, increasing the danger to all. This describes numerous crowd disasters. It also illustrates the financial crisis of 2008.

The recent crisis is a story of mass ignorance. It deserves to be treated as a powerful lesson on the importance of information transparency in a market economy and, by extension, on the crucial role to be played by a free press. We learned the hard way that without transparency, markets not only fail to fulfill their primary function in allocating capital efficiently but also can become agents of destruction.

Unfortunately, in the five years since, it is not at all clear we have removed such risks. Despite reams of new regulations and information technology aimed at opening up the financial markets to more scrutiny, financial firms are finding new and creative ways to retain and control information and thus are undermining the functioning of markets. Many governments, meanwhile, are limiting disclosure about their economies. And this is happening as newsrooms in developed countries continue to shrink, making rigorous, independent investigative reporting into banking practices and markets all the more difficult just when it is needed most.

From former U.S. Federal Reserve Chairman Alan Greenspan down, financial policymakers in the late 1990s and the first seven years of this century believed that technological innovation was making markets more efficient, open, and fair. It was widely contended that the advent of electronic trading had created a more transparent marketplace and had eaten into the power of Wall Street's bond and stock traders. By some measures this was true. The broadcasting of asset prices across networks such as Bloomberg's meant that banks were less able to exploit investor ignorance when buying and selling securities; it became more difficult for them to buy stocks, bonds, or other financial assets at a steep discount and sell them at a much higher price.

But technology can also make markets *less* transparent. The expansion of computing power, coupled with a soft regulatory environment, allowed Wall Street banks and other powerful institutions to add opacity back into the financial system and to put themselves in the middle of a new, phenomenally complex investment business. Leveraging their unmatchable capacity to pay high salaries, the banks lured math and physics experts into their fold. These "quants" were put to work engineering an alphabet soup of highly complicated financial instruments that were snapped up by an investor community hungry for new ways to turn their cash into profits.

The more complex these newfangled products became, the further detached they were from the underlying risk in their component assets— which in many cases came down to the prospect of an American homeowner falling behind on monthly mortgage payments. This made it harder for an outsider to figure out how to price them. What's more, thanks to special exemptions from regulatory oversight, most of them traded not on traditional exchanges such as the London Stock Exchange or the Chicago Board of Trade but in over-the-counter markets where prices, volumes, and other transaction details are unavailable to outsiders. This meant that neither the investing public nor regulators had an accurate sense of the huge buildup of risks being taken by the biggest players.

"We live in a world where there is so much information, and where technology has flattened the information hierarchy. So, in theory, everybody has easy access to everything and yet you still have" enormous secrecy in markets, said Alan Murray, president of the Pew Research Center and a former deputy managing editor of *The Wall Street Journal*. "What you saw in the crisis was . . . that people may have had access to information, but if we can't access it in a way that anybody understands then it doesn't make a difference."

Wall Street banks were greatly empowered before the crisis, aided by their role in developing the complex new financial instruments that fueled the credit bubble, which gave them exclusive access to the complicated formulas on which those instruments were priced. This enterprise was spectacularly successful in restoring the banks' monopoly over information, helping them overcome the challenges to profitability posed by electronic trading and allowing top bankers to claim annual compensation deals that in some cases ran higher than $100 million.

To be fair, those on the losing side of Wall Street's profit-driven pre-crisis trade mostly failed to exploit new opportunities to expose the risks associated with it. In this era of "big data," where high-tech analytical techniques can produce abundant, quantifiable information, we should all have been empowered to uncover the truth. But in reality, for the average investor, journalist, or even regulator, this new trove of data has been mostly out of reach and unintelligible.

It should now be the duty of journalists to unlock it. And to do so, they need to harness the same tools that financial institutions and corporations use to sift, interpret, and make sense of mass digital information. The value of human sources providing information on market players' activities hasn't gone away—think of the lasting impact of *The Wall Street Journal's* "London Whale" scoop on JPMorgan Chase's risky trading bets last year, a story that led to news that the bank had racked up $6 billion in losses and, later, $1 billion in regulatory fines. But those stories must now be complemented with computer-enhanced analysis and interpretation. To get at the truth will require crunching the numbers—billions of them.

"The question is: How do you take the proliferation of data and extract something intelligent out of it?" said the Pew Center's Murray. "I think data analysis is going to become a much more important part of journalism."

If journalists are to investigate and interpret the complex systems of data management with which financial institutions create information monopolies, they need resources. Yet in the developed countries in which these complex new financial markets are thriving, the dominant trend in the penny-pinching media industry is for cutbacks, not investment, as traditional news outlets adjust to a highly competitive environment for online advertising. According to the Pew Center's annual State of the Media report, in 2012 the total U.S. newsroom workforce dipped below 40,000 for the first time since 1978, a 30 percent decline since 2000. Similar challenges exist in Europe, where the same patterns of declining newspaper revenue and media fragmentation were evident in a seminal 10-year study by the Reuters Institute in 2012.

Such statistics are depressing enough, but they take on new relevance when positioned against another one: The total number of public relations managers and specialists in the U.S. stood at 320,000 in 2010 and was projected to grow by 21 percent in 2020, according to the U.S. Bureau of Labor Statistics. That's well above the projected growth rate of the overall national workforce. In other words, there's a growing and well-funded demand for those who deliver spin in the interest of corporate entities and a declining demand for those whose job is to independently report and analyze those entities' activities without bias.

Hard data on the number of journalists becoming public relations agents is difficult to come by. But anyone in the financial press—where the prospects of being lured to a corporate communications job are greatest—will recognize a trend. They know that the often higher salaries offered on what journalists call the "dark side" are enticing struggling reporters and editors away from journalism. Some even compare it to Washington's revolving-door problem, where politicians and their aides are increasingly hired as lobbyists at the end of their public service careers, creating a conflicted relationship that tightens corporate money's stranglehold on politics. The comparable concern is that the possibility of future job opportunities compromises business journalists' ability to keep an arm's-length relationship with their sources.

"The world of journalism is losing a lot of brainpower and experience that is going over to work for corporate America. To me that is troublesome," said Chris Roush, a journalism professor at the University of North Carolina at Chapel Hill and the founder of the *Talking Biz News* blog, a clearinghouse of news about staff movements and other developments in financial journalism.

Here's another complicating factor: In the post-crisis era, governments around the world have become far bigger players in world markets and economies, a direct outcome of the financial rescue missions many had to undertake. The problem is they are not being forthcoming with information—certainly not to the press.

The U.S. Federal Reserve, whose policies of boosting the supply of money to stimulate the economy and whose accumulated stockpile of $3.6 trillion in purchased bonds have left global investors singularly absorbed by its policy deliberations, launched some effective pro-transparency initiatives throughout this period. For one, Chairman Ben Bernanke now gives news conferences after the Federal Reserve's regular meetings to set monetary policy. But it hasn't been entirely transparent, either. The Federal Reserve fought hard against Freedom of Information Act requests from Fox Business and Bloomberg that sought the names of the institutions that received $3.3 trillion in emergency central bank funding in the fall of 2008. Even after the Supreme Court ruled that the Fed must release the data, it delivered it in a rudimentary and hard-to-interpret format.

The other behemoth in world finance is the Chinese government. With $3.7 trillion in foreign currency reserves, the country's central bank, the People's Bank of China, has an almost unmatched capacity to move markets whenever it tweaks the mix of foreign bonds it holds. The problem is that beyond reporting an estimate of total holdings, China reveals virtually nothing about what it does with those funds. Beijing refuses even to comply with a program run by the International Monetary Fund that reports a simple breakdown of different national reserve managers' currency allocations, even though a lengthy delay in that report's release means the information is hardly sensitive. There are also serious doubts about the quality of economic data in China, the second-largest economy in the world. That is exacerbating fear of a future economic crisis brought on by excessive debt. Chinese banks and foreign investors are owed hundreds of billions of dollars by local and provincial governments that partook in a decade-long construction binge.

It has been a better story in most other emerging markets, where waves of reforms since the Cold War and the adoption of websites for publishing official statistics have generally encouraged a more open approach to economic information. But the crisis-like environment since 2008 has put those changes at risk, as volatile flows of speculative money in and out of these smaller economies have left some questioning the value of playing by the international community's transparency rules. Some have already crossed that line. Argentina's government, for example, has significantly understated inflation statistics over the past six years—based on numerous independent studies, including by the IMF. It has fined economists who have produced more accurate measures of price trends and has implicitly threatened news organizations that reproduced those independent estimates. In a move that opposition politicians likened to the intimidation tactics of Argentina's Dirty War, a judge presiding over the government's case against the economists ordered newspapers to divulge personal information about journalists who covered inflation.

This is to say nothing of how entrenched corrupt practices and conflicts of interest undermine financial journalism in many countries, with blame found on both sides of the business–media relationship. In Indonesia, for example, some local news organizations have turned a blind eye to the biases encouraged by "envelope journalism," as their reporters often supplement their meager incomes with the envelopes of cash that are stuffed into public-relations packets at corporate news conferences. And in various places where journalists do strive for hard-hitting, independent reporting about powerful business elites, they can run the risk of legal harassment, violence, or even murder. For example, in 2012, Cambodian journalist Hang Serei Odom was found murdered with ax wounds to his head after having reported on military involvement in illegal logging. All of this diminishes the quality of information available to the public about the state of the local economy and financial system, which in turn breeds inefficiencies and crises.

Press freedom and information transparency are arguably even more urgently needed now in the world of business than before the crisis. That's because the same kinds of institutions that created the conditions for the 2008 meltdown are up to their old tricks. Continuing a decades-long pattern of counter-responding to regulation and technological change with its own innovations, Wall Street will protect its profit base. Some argue that if the financial markets hadn't done so over the years, society's natural demand for an open, transparent marketplace would by now have rendered banking an unsexy, low-margin business.

"The search for non-transparent markets was more of a reflection of the weakness of the banks' business models. They could only make money in the dark," said Terry Connelly, dean emeritus of Golden Gate University, who worked at Salomon Smith Barney in the 1980s, a time when that bank's bond traders established a reputation for trail-blazing financial engineering.

Algorithmic, high-frequency trading is one new area of concern. With this technology, Wall Street banks and hedge funds exploit what

Connelly calls "the opaqueness of time." These ultra-fast trading operations employ computerized trading systems that process information and execute multiple buy-and-sell trades within milliseconds. All this happens within a time frame that a human brain is incapable of even contemplating, let alone monitoring. Once again, innovation has edged out transparency.

High-frequency trading has thrived off the expansion and digitalization of financial information—the stock prices, economic statistics, and corporate earnings reports that are entered into the algorithms. Enabled by the ever-widening information base, high-frequency trading systems grew so large that by 2010 they accounted for 56 percent of all U.S. stock-trading volume and 77 percent of the U.K. market, according to estimates from the Tabb Group, a consulting group.

Its proponents tout high-speed trading as a driver of market efficiency, but that has been brought into question by a string of sudden market breakdowns, including the "flash crash" of 2010, when an avalanche of self-perpetuating sell orders for U.S. stocks turned a relatively stable market into a scene of chaos in which $1 trillion in market value was temporarily wiped out. A common view now is that high-frequency trading is at best beneficial only to investors with the most powerful computer systems and is at worst a destabilizing force capable of unleashing a scary form of automated herd behavior.

Meanwhile, alternative electronic trading platforms and quasi-exchanges have created new venues for big investors to execute trades in secret. Trading services known as "dark pools" invite large institutions to place and execute orders anonymously and outside the purview of regulated financial exchanges. Again, the advantages accrue to the biggest and most well-financed firms, all at the expense of individuals and of pension funds, whose charters require them to invest transparently on traditional exchanges.

Regulators are trying to curb these abuses. But the complex set of rules developed under the 2010 Dodd-Frank Act—2,300 pages of initial legislation, which in turn gave rise to 155 new rules contained in 14,000 pages of regulations—is not an elegant solution. Historically, a basic principle behind market regulation in the U.S. was that rule-making should prioritize the enforcement of transparency so that more draconian constraints on investment activity aren't needed. Freedom of information, it was thought, would facilitate free markets. One could argue, then, that the Dodd-Frank Act, with its unseemly mix of excessive bureaucracy and negotiated loopholes, reflects a failure of those past efforts to achieve financial transparency. A truly open and free market in which information is widely available to all participants would not give rise to the abuses that prompt such heavy-handed intervention. Yale Law Professor Jonathan Macey even contends that the regulations can undermine transparency and honesty in the financial sector because banking firms cease to worry about bad press. With the government now promising to protect Wall Street's clients, "an industry that was built on reputation now could (not) care less about its reputation," he told *The Wall Street Journal*.

One area in which Dodd-Frank does free up information is in its regulation of so-called swaps, financial instruments that give investors the opportunity to transfer the risks attached to certain securities to other investors. One version, the credit-default swap, was a key contributor to the financial crisis. That's because the over-the-counter market on which they traded provided too little information about the interconnected risks of default in the financial system. It meant no one could perceive the domino effect that would arise once a large institution like Lehman Brothers failed to make payments—a development that led each market participant to respond with an excess of caution, dumping bonds, demanding repayments from their borrowers, and charging more for insurance against default, until credit completely dried up. To mitigate the threat of such mass panic attacks, Dodd-Frank rules now force many of these instruments to trade in more public forums known as swap execution facilities. With the prices, volumes, and terms of the swaps contracts more transparently presented, the hope is that investors and regulators have a clearer picture of the overall market and its potential for a 2008-style "systemic" meltdown. Ultimately, the goal is to make a "crowd disaster" less likely.

It will take the next debt crisis—and whether it generates a wider threat to the financial system—to determine whether these changes have removed systemic risk from the swaps market. But what is known is that Wall Street lobbyists successfully fought to water down some of these new regulations. For one, most currency swaps, a growing portion of the $4 trillion-a-day global foreign exchange market, were exempted from trading on the more transparent swap execution facilities. Meanwhile, U.S. banks aligned themselves with European governments to convince U.S. regulators that overseas transactions could continue to occur in over-the-counter markets. The banks argued that without these adjustments, the uncertainty imposed on markets could have fueled another credit crunch and that businesses needed the customizable strategies for hedging risk available in over-the-counter markets. Nonetheless, the upshot is that much of the global derivatives market still operates outside the new open trading rules. The opaque system survives.

Given these failings, more regulation could be on its way. The authorities in the U.S. are increasingly concerned, for example, that owners of high-speed trading systems can access and act upon sensitive market-moving information—including closely guarded government data—ahead of human traders. Any effort to address this imbalance should not, however, infringe upon the right of the press to freely report that information. It is in society's interest that the guiding principle again be one where regulation works to enhance transparency instead of discouraging risk-taking.

Perhaps the biggest challenges lie within our industry. We journalists must lead the struggle for more transparency in finance. But to do that effectively, we'll need to reverse the decline in news organizations' resources. The fundamental challenge in developed economies is to make financial news sufficiently profitable for serious media groups to attract reporters and editors of integrity and talent and to invest in technology that empowers them. Meanwhile, as emerging economies develop more sophisticated financial markets, it's important that journalists are granted the freedom and technology to report on them.

As a starting point to addressing these challenges it's worth acknowledging the central theme here: that in a market economy, information is extremely valuable. Investors need fast, reliable information from a trustworthy source whose interests are not conflicted. Why wouldn't they pay for that?

Media companies feel trapped by Internet competition that's strengthening the bargaining power of their advertising clients and reducing spot news to a commodity. But given the market's insatiable demand for reliable information, there is intrinsic value in their newsrooms' output. Unlocking it is a noble task, one that would align many interests: those of investors who seek to profit from knowledge; those of society, for which transparent, efficient markets are vital to prosperity; and those of journalists, who deserve to be fairly rewarded for a valuable service.

*Michael J. Casey is a senior columnist covering economics and global financial markets at* The Wall Street Journal. *He has worked as a journalist in Australia, Thailand, Indonesia, Argentina, and the United States. He is the author of two books,* The Unfair Trade *and* Che's Afterlife. *This commentary reflects his opinions and not necessarily the opinions of* Dow Jones *or* The Wall Street Journal.

# 3

# THE FRONT LINES

# Syrian Journalists Strive to Report, Despite Shifting Dangers

*By María Salazar-Ferro*

Journalists Bryn Karcha, center, of Canada, and Toshifumi Fujimoto, right, of Japan, run for cover with an unidentified fixer in Aleppo's district of Salaheddine on December 29, 2012.

*Source:* Reuters/Muzaffar Salman.

S yria is the most dangerous country in the world for reporters and yet, every day, hundreds of its citizens risk their lives to shoot photos, record video, and file reports on the civil conflict. Many are trying to reach the international community. Others want to raise the level of awareness on the ground. Most fear that without their work, the conflict's atrocities will go undocumented. And some say they do it because, in war, there is no other work.

Since the beginning of the uprising in March 2011, Syrian and foreign journalists and media workers have been targeted, research by the Committee to Protect Journalists (CPJ) shows. At least 51 have been killed in retaliation for their work, and at least 30 others were missing, as of November 2013. Early on, the government of President Bashar al-Assad barred the international press while its security forces arrested and brutalized dozens of local news gatherers. Rebel forces counterattacked—targeting journalists and outlets believed to be pro-government. By late 2011, journalists faced yet a third front with the appearance on the battleground of non-Syrian Islamist militant groups that have attacked, abducted, and killed them.

A local independent press movement has grown in the midst of this chaos, and today, while no verified number exists, CPJ research shows that scores of Syrian outlets are actively reporting. "Prior to the revolution there was only one story being told: the story that the regime wanted to tell," said Mowaffaq Safadi, an exiled Syrian journalist in Turkey. "Now, even if the media is not all professional, at least we have our different stories being told."

Syria's president inherited the job from his authoritarian father, Hafez al-Assad, who ruled Syria from 1971 until his death in 2000. Until then, only news outlets run by the government or affiliated with the ruling Arab Socialist Baath Party were allowed to publish. When the younger Assad came to power, there was some initial hope for change, and the local press took its first tentative steps toward greater independence and more open criticism. However, a 2001 press law that legalized private publications—banned since 1963—also maintained severe restrictions. It required all private publications to be licensed by the government, and prohibited them from reporting on military affairs or topics that could "harm" national security or "national unity." Violators faced up to three years in prison and heavy fines.

With these restrictions in place, some independent online websites began to flourish in the early 2000s, according to Massoud Akko, a Syrian who monitors the country's press freedom from Norway and bills himself as a media activist. These early blogs, Akko said in a telephone interview, focused on general news and politics. "People used them to issue their opinions," he said. But the government began to filter online dissent, blocked politically sensitive sites, and detained bloggers. Online self-censorship became pervasive and, in 2009, CPJ placed Syria third on a list of the 10 worst countries worldwide for bloggers.

Then came the euphoria of the Arab Spring. As spreading dissent in the region bubbled up in Syria—inspiring vast public demonstrations in the first half of 2011—a makeshift, independent media began to surface. Its members, however, were not all professional journalists. Instead, most say they are citizens swept up by the revolution, or revolutionaries who took on the role of news gatherers as a contribution to Syria's political change. They call themselves citizen journalists, media workers, or media activists.

"The revolution was a very emotional moment for everyone, including me, and it was natural to want to join the protests," Safadi told CPJ. "I decided to start filming the protests because what you saw on Syrian news was ridiculous, it was insulting. Filming was the natural thing for me to do to tell the story of what was happening. So I started filming and uploading what I was finding to YouTube."

International reporters swarmed the country as the initial protests intensified. But by the end of March 2011, the government had begun its crackdown, expelling journalists, barring others from entering, and forcing outlets to shut down operations, making Syrians on the ground even more anxious to spread the word.

Many Syrians, who like Safadi had nominal media abilities but access to mobile phones, cameras, or the Internet, improvised as journalists. In March 2011, Omar Alkhani had just returned to Syria from years abroad with the hope of starting his own marketing firm. He told CPJ that as the first demonstrations erupted in his Damascus neighborhood, his impulse was to take photos. Eventually he created a Facebook page dedicated to documenting the uprising. "I began alone," Alkhani said. "But as only one person I could not cover everything, so I asked friends who had skills to help me, and as things started to get bigger, we started a union for people working with the revolution who were working to coordinate demonstrations and to cover what was happening."

Dozens of similar groups began popping up across Syria, *The New York Times* reported in June 2011. Most were conceived as social media–centric groups that organized protests. But the need grew to spread information to Syrians and the outside world, first about the protests and then about the government reprisals, and so these groups turned into de-facto news agencies that remained deeply involved in the politics of the revolution.

Known as coordination committees, media centers, press centers, or media unions, these mostly informal alliances continue to operate in parts of Syria. Journalists working with media centers publish information on social media, or file stories to independent online Syrian radio stations or news blogs. Some media centers working in rebel-controlled areas are able to publish ad-hoc magazines with succinct information on the conflict, economic and social issues, and general news. They print about 300 copies at once, and publish sporadically. Other Syrian journalists work independently of media centers and file directly to Syrian or international outlets abroad.

■ ■ ■

Media centers remain decentralized and mostly function autonomously. Their members work out of residential spaces, using a few laptops, cameras, and printers, and the essential tools they need to get online. "It's not hard to get your hands on these things," said Rami Jarrah, an award-winning journalist who co-manages the citizen press group ANA News Media Association. "It's just dangerous."

It is not always clear where financial backing for Syrian outlets and media centers comes from. It is believed some support comes from international organizations, foreign governments, and individual donations. Private donors, Jarrah said, are Syrians outside the country or people in neighboring countries, who give small sums to cover the costs of setting up and paying for satellite Internet connections, or who directly donate laptops, cameras, and other equipment.

With the war well into its third year, the dangers for journalists have multiplied since the appearance of the first media centers in the spring of 2011. Then, it seemed the Assad government was the primary obstacle to those seeking to document the uprising. Now, the kinds of threats journalists face daily differ depending on where they are and which armed faction controls the area, said Razan Ghazzawi, a Syria-based blogger and former press freedom campaigner. She was arrested in 2011 for her writing and in 2012 for her activism on behalf of the Syrian Center for Media and Freedom of Expression.

According to the U.S.-born Ghazzawi, there is constant turmoil as the revolution's many antagonists maneuver for control. And according to Jarrah, "There is a complete shift on the ground all the time. Every day there are several battles going on, and at the end of the day each battle has changed something. So it is impossible to know who is controlling what."

Government-controlled areas remain almost impossible for independent journalists to work in, said Ghazzawi. The government controls everything, including communications and the streets. "You cannot have a camera in the street or lift your mobile. It's a very high security situation and you are subject to arrest," Jarrah said. "Citizen journalists arrested are never heard from again." Journalists working in these areas do so very discreetly, sending their work for publication outside Syria through a variety of communication channels.

Many, according to Jarrah, have government links or jobs, and file secretly. Their motivation: "To expose the crimes that are being committed by the regime," Jarrah told CPJ. "Their information can have a big impact."

Though it is still very difficult for international reporters to enter Syria, the Assad government allowed more foreign correspondents into the country after it agreed to a Russian-American plan in September 2013 to destroy Syria's chemical weapons to avert American airstrikes. Who is allowed in remains arbitrary and personalized. But the vast majority of those who obtain visas work under constant surveillance and tight restrictions in government-controlled areas. A few international journalists still sneak over the border to report without authorization.

According to Ghazzawi, Syrian journalists working in rebel-controlled areas, which she and others call "liberated," have the most freedom, though they work under the constant threat of shelling and other forms of indiscriminate attacks. In these areas, media centers continue to operate, often with protection from rebel authorities. Open criticism of rebel groups and actions, however, is not always tolerated, and CPJ has documented several attacks on journalists and outlets perceived to support the government. Tolerance from Free Syria Army (FSA) fighters, Jarrah said, tends to depend on the battalion.

Then, there are the multiple battlegrounds where not only are the government forces and the FSA fighting for domination, but also such extremist groups as the Al-Qaeda affiliated Islamic State of Iraq and al-Sham (ISIS). Journalists say it is very difficult to physically report in areas where there are continuous battles and a clear lack of basic infrastructure. According to Ghazzawi, journalists working there often lose their tools—laptops or Internet accessing equipment—to shelling, or they are forced to abandon them as they hastily change locations.

Contested areas where extremist groups have control, even temporarily, are particularly dangerous. Syrian and foreign journalists have consistently been kidnapped and brutalized. "Where there are Islamist groups like ISIS, it's very similar to where the regime is," said Jarrah, whose news agency has been targeted and has had at least one reporter who was kidnapped. "But the regime remains more dangerous for citizen journalists because while ISIS and other groups don't arrest everyone, and discriminate based on who attacks them and who doesn't, the regime does not."

Akko, the media activist, agrees that security varies from area to area, though he says other concerns are universal. One such concern is getting paid. Journalists working only with media centers are rarely compensated. Rather, they offer their material and information freely online. Others, who have gained more experience, freelance for regional outlets or the Syrian media based abroad. According to Akko, those who freelance work for small sums. He estimates that on average Syrian independent media and regional Arab outlets pay individual journalists US$50 per article, regardless of the security situation. According to Italian journalist Francesca Borri, foreign freelancers willing to sneak into the country are paid as little as US$70 per piece. The truth, says Akko, is that most journalists working on the ground in Syria are not paid.

Basic security concerns are also shared by most. The greatest requirement for journalists in Syria remains the ability to shift locations at a moment's notice to avoid capture and incarceration or, worse, death. Many journalists who spoke to CPJ cited as a turning point the February 2012 attack on a press center in Homs that killed American reporter Marie Colvin and French photographer Rémi Ochlik. Though the deaths occurred on the 19th consecutive day of shelling by Assad forces on the Baba Amr neighborhood, many believe that they were not a coincidence but the result of a targeted attack on the journalists, who had huddled in the improvised office. Speculation varies on whether it was the satellite phones or the Internet signal at the center that helped pinpoint their location. But to the local media, the lesson was clear: Technological tools can get the news out, but they can also leave a clear and dangerous trail.

Jarrah said "tough lessons" like the one from Baba Amr make up the unofficial guidelines of Syria's independent press. Journalists "learn how to work the hard way," he told CPJ. "When they see colleagues get arrested because of a mistake they made, they avoid repeating it."

Akko agrees that, so far, mistakes have been the most effective teaching tools, though journalists have also organized online and face-to-face training sessions. At these meetings, those who have more experience share basic information with those who are starting out. The training differs, according to Akko, a professional journalist and active member of the Syrian Journalist Association, a civil society group created in 2012 to build independent journalism and monitor press freedom in Syria.

Most often the training focuses on digital and physical security, but it can also include information on journalistic ethics, writing structure, and camera angles. Despite the good faith effort, Akko believes that these workshops are not sufficient to strengthen the news-gathering work that is being done in Syria.

International non-governmental organizations have also organized workshops outside the country that touch on many of the same subjects. However, journalists who spoke to CPJ remain uncertain about whether these are having any real impact. Mostly, they worry that the knowledge gained abroad by journalists and activists in exile, as well as some who travel in and out of the country, does not make its way back into Syria. "There is something wrong in the delivery of the training," said Alkhani, the marketing entrepreneur turned chronicler of the revolt. "It's always the same people who are doing [them], and always the same people who are attending. So there is a real problem because the information is not getting to the people who really need it."

In general, Syrian journalists said that the efforts of the international community to support them have been off track. "A journalist is a journalist even if he is Syrian, Dutch, French or American," Akko said. "No one is really talking about our journalists. And there should be more of a focus on the situation of the journalists who are working inside Syria." Though none of the journalists interviewed by CPJ made specific suggestions, all agreed that the international community needed to devote more resources to supporting the work Syrians are doing.

An additional problem for the professional growth of Syria's independent press, according to Akko, is the continuing flight of experienced journalists, many of whom once worked for the government-controlled news outlets. Since the conflict began, the writers, newscasters and others working for the government-controlled media have fled en masse, taking their considerable knowledge and experience with them. By CPJ's count, more than 70 Syrian journalists have left since 2011, although others put their numbers higher.

Many, like Rania Badri, the former host of a popular morning talk show on a radio station owned by the Assad family, worked for government media and quit their jobs to join foreign or independent media outlets. Badri left the country shortly after resigning and started a short-lived independent radio station that reported Syrian news from abroad. It was closed because of continued threats. She now lives in Paris and no longer works as a journalist.

Those forced into exile include citizen journalists. Most fled through Jordan, Lebanon, or Egypt, and settled in Turkey, where their legal situation remains vague. In October 2011, the Turkish government extended "temporary protection" to all Syrian refugees, but journalists based there have said they live in a sort of limbo, unclear how long official protection will last.

Most of the international press corps seems to have left Syria as well. After several killings and a succession of kidnappings, which spiked in 2013, fewer foreign journalists and outlets are willing to take the chances required to report from Syria. International nongovernmental media groups, like the London-based Rory Peck Trust, have published cautionary statements urging foreign freelancers to stay away. And journalists themselves have publically questioned whether the story is worth the risk. "It would be unwise (at best) and irresponsible (at worst) to go inside Syria as an independent journalist at this time," award-winning photojournalist Javier Manzano told the Rory Peck Trust in August 2013.

Yet, as the most experienced news gatherers withdraw from the field, the explosion of people reporting from Syria and outlets disseminating information continues to grow. Consistently, journalists who spoke to CPJ said there is no way of knowing how many Syrian outlets exist today. The overall landscape includes hundreds of radio stations that broadcast online and a handful on FM; more than a dozen newspapers and a few magazines that publish informally inside Syria with help from local committees or rebel groups; and myriad websites, blogs, and social media pages. The quality of content and analysis and their political affiliations vary.

For security reasons, many outlets born in the early stages of the revolution have moved their operations abroad, mostly to southern Turkey. From the border, groups like Jarrah's ANA, as well as individual journalists, have easy access to information from sources inside the country and from the continuous flow of refugees. Most important, they are well positioned to hop over the border to report.

Alkhani, the marketing specialist turned photographer, worked from southern Turkey for several months. He told CPJ that in March 2013, as the crisis grew worse in the capital, he left Damascus for Antakya in Turkey. By then, his photos had gained some notice, and he had freelanced for Reuters, Demotix, and other agencies. From Turkey, Alkhani said, he easily entered Syria on a weekly basis to report.

Alkhani said he also provided others helping the rebel cause with additional services, and in August 2013, he agreed to help an international organization smuggle equipment to access the Internet into Syria. On his way back, Alkhani was stopped outside Aleppo by a group of armed individuals. He was held for 35 days by fighters he suspected of being ISIS members. "They gave me five charges," Alkhani said in a phone interview. "One for doing photography; two, for helping foreign journalists, infidels, get into the country; three, for being a Satan worshipper because of videos they found on my laptop; four, for adultery because my wife is Christian; and, five, for not supporting the Islamist State. Every time a charge was delivered, I was tortured."

The photographer said over the course of his abduction, his captors whipped him repeatedly while threatening him with worse violence. Alkhani said everything he had with him was confiscated, including his laptop, camera, iPad, and some money. When he was finally released, the photographer was driven, blindfolded, back to the Turkish border, where he was told to get on a bus out of Syria. "They didn't say why they were releasing me," Alkhani said. "But they did Shariah Law on me, and they took all my stuff, so I could not work anymore."

Most of the news outlets operating from abroad tend to rely on networks of journalists inside Syria. According to Jarrah, ANA's network of reporters is made up of friends of friends, or friends of relatives who can provide information on daily events in their neighborhoods. "We seek them," Jarrah said. "They don't seek us, because there are too many outlets competing. We seek them, we vet them, and we decide whether to get information from them." One of the main qualities Jarrah said ANA looks for is objectivity, and therefore it prefers reporters with few links to political networks, or activists without real ties to the revolution.

But objectivity, others say, is very hard to come by at a point when those who are reporting on the Syrian war are also those who have been living it for several years. "Those working today are a mixture of people who are suffering, have personal aspirations, and are facing personal circumstances that show in their work," said Safadi, in a Skype interview from a café in Istanbul. "Although they are motivated to provide essential information from inside Syria, they are exposed emotionally, and they are connected to what's happening personally. It's hard to stop and have the objectivity needed to report."

*Daniel DeFreia*, *CPJ's 2013–2014 Steiger Fellow, and* **Jason Stern**, *research associate for CPJ's Middle East and North Africa program, contributed reporting.*

*María Salazar-Ferro*, *CPJ's Impunity Campaign and Journalist Assistance Program coordinator, reports on exiled and missing journalists, and has represented CPJ on missions to Mexico and the Philippines, among others.*

# Finding the Courage to Cover Sexual Violence

*By Frank Smyth*

**Women march for justice and security in New Delhi on January 2, 2013, following the funeral of a student who died after being gang-raped.**

*Source:* Reuters/Adnan Abidi.

A sensitive if not taboo subject in much of the world, sexual violence often goes unreported. Covering sexual assault, including rape, can bring swift and unpredictable repercussions, leaving many journalists and others torn over how best to navigate the risks.

"You don't have the courage. You don't want to get into trouble," Chi Yvonne Leina, an award-winning Cameroonian journalist and contributor to the women's activist network World Pulse, told CPJ. "What you are reporting, who you are, can lead to changes in the way the community sees you," she said. World Pulse describes itself as a network using digital media in more than 190 countries to connect women worldwide and give them a global voice.

But attitudes can change. In India, a fatal gang-rape case in Delhi in December 2012 ended up generating more coverage in Indian newspapers, on television news and commentary programs, and in social media forums than ever before. Four men were eventually convicted of the crime and sentenced to death. Their lawyers have filed an appeal. The media coverage and the case itself have, by all accounts, helped reshape attitudes about sexual violence. "The way girls think now has changed dramatically after this particular case," Urmila Chanam, a columnist in northeastern India for the English daily newspaper *Sangai Express*, told CPJ.

Anyone reporting on sexual violence needs to be mindful of the potential risks not only to themselves, but also to the victims of the attacks.

"Think about the safety of the witnesses and sources," Abdiaziz Abdinuur, a Somali journalist who was forced into exile after reporting on sexual assaults, told CPJ.

"We could do more damage," said Chanam. Reporting sexual violence "disturbs the cultural elements in our country," she explained. Yet Chanam, who is another World Pulse contributor, ultimately wants "every case to be reported." She said that she gives the choice to the victim whether to report an individual case of rape, while collaborating more broadly with activists to change the way people perceive sexual violence.

Sometimes reporters pay a price for covering sexual attacks and their aftermaths. In July 2012, some Indian journalists were tipped off that a large group of men in Mangalore were chasing, beating, and groping teenage women at a local birthday party. The assailants were Hindu fundamentalists apparently upset at the way the women were associating with men. One local television journalist, Naveen Soorinje, called the police and filmed the scene. His subsequent TV report accused the police of responding slowly to his repeated calls about the attack.

Soorinje's footage was used to identify dozens of suspects. But four months after the episode, Soorinje was himself charged with participating in the attack. He spent four months in jail until his release in March 2013. The Committee to Protect Journalists considers the arrest to be retaliatory.

Just over a week after the 2012 gang rape on a bus in Delhi of a 23-year-old female physiotherapy student, the police in Imphal shot and killed Dwijamani Singh, a reporter for a regional satellite television network, as he was covering protests against sexual assaults of women. The protesters were demonstrating against both the Delhi gang-rape attack and a more recent gang rape of an actress in Imphal. Singh was killed as the police opened fire when some protesters turned violent, according to news reports.

Attitudes about sexual attacks in India remain mixed. In the Delhi gang-rape case, pressure from the girl's parents and the nation's press gave the case unprecedented attention, which helped lead to arrests. In what seemed like a reaction to the widespread media coverage, a lower court barred journalists from covering the "fast-track" trial for two months.

But the press continued to clash with the authorities throughout the trial. In March, the Delhi High Court lifted the ban on reporters, although some restrictions remained, including allowing only one journalist from each accredited media organization into the courtroom, and prohibiting journalists from publishing the names of the victim or witnesses. In April, the judge presiding over the case arbitrarily barred a British journalist for *The Independent* in London from covering the trial.

Attitudes about gender in India along with the economic implications for families may help explain why covering sexual violence can be such a challenge for the press. Attitudes toward women are "the core reasons" behind both the nation's sexual assaults and why they are so often kept in the dark, said Chanam of the *Sangai Express*. "It starts before birth."

Girls are considered less valuable than boys, she said, and selective abortions of female fetuses are common. For every 1,000 boys,

836 girls are born in India, according to a study using birth data as late as 2005 published in *The Lancet*. The families of a young female rape victim may also pay an economic price if the crime is made public, Chanam said. Most Indian marriages are still arranged, and the bride's family is expected to pay a dowry to the groom's family. The family of an unmarried woman who has been raped often does not want it made public, she explained, because that would only make it harder and more expensive for her to marry.

In many nations, a gender-based sense of "honor" is another reason why sexual violence is often kept out of the press. Publicity around a rape case "can be extremely dangerous for the rape victims themselves," said Soroya Chemaly, a freelance feminist writer for various news outlets, including *The Huffington Post*.

Afghanistan is one nation where a family's honor, or its perception, helps keep sexual assaults from being reported. "Afghans are very sensitive about honor," Ali Shahidy, a writer and women's rights activist who has since left Afghanistan for the United States, told CPJ. If a woman in the family is sexually assaulted, he said, "they keep it as close as they can to protect their honor."

Such attitudes span the globe. "Sometimes you don't want to identify the victims to protect the victims," Achieng Beatrice Nas, an activist and World Pulse contributor from Uganda, told CPJ. "Sometimes you don't identify the victim to protect yourself."

But there's another reason why crimes of sexual violence may go unreported. Government security forces are among the most common culprits in sexual violence, according to Lauren Wolfe, an award-winning journalist and director of the Women Under Siege Project, a New York-based nonprofit group that documents rape and other forms of sexual violence in conflict areas. "Most people we talk to won't speak about it because they're too scared," said Wolfe, who has helped document sexual violence in Afghanistan, Kashmir, Sudan, and Syria. While CPJ's senior editor, Wolfe wrote the CPJ report, "The Silencing Crime: Sexual Violence and Journalists."

Sexism and misogyny also play a role in keeping sexual assault stories from being reported, Chemaly said. "Male entitlement" is at the root of the challenges reporters face covering sexual violence, she said, because some men feel "they have the right to abuse, the right to rape."

A study published in September 2013 in *The Lancet* based on interviews with men in Asian and Pacific nations noted a "high rape prevalence" that "is probably rooted in aspects of culture related to sexual entitlement and sex relations."

In January 2013, Al-Jazeera's English-language TV channel aired a report alleging that government soldiers in Somalia had raped women in refugee camps in Mogadishu. A few days later, the Somali freelance journalist Abdinuur pursued the same line of investigation and interviewed a woman who said she had been raped by soldiers. Abdinuur was promptly arrested to face a series of charges including "offending state institutions" and "false reporting," even though he had never published any report based on the interview.

The police arrested the woman he interviewed, initially charging her with similar crimes. The authorities also questioned, but did not charge, Omar Faruk, a correspondent for Al-Jazeera's Arabic service in Somalia. Abdinuur was finally released more than two months later, when the Supreme Court dismissed all charges. He fled to Uganda. "I was arrested," he later said in an audio interview with CPJ, "because of interviewing rape victims."

CPJ archives include a number of other cases of journalists' enduring reprisals after covering stories of sexual attacks. In 2000 in Kakamega, Kenya, two journalists from the daily newspaper, *The People*, were arrested and interrogated for hours for reporting that police officers had sexually assaulted three local women. In 2001, in Sri Lanka, A.S.M. Fasmi, a reporter with a Tamil-language newspaper, was detained and interrogated by intelligence agents after reporting a story about the rape of two women by security forces.

In 2006, Mexican journalist and activist Lydia Cacho was subjected to a trumped-up criminal defamation suit along with threats of violence. Tapes of telephone conversations between several people, including the then-governor of the state of Puebla and a local businessman, were delivered to the Mexico City offices of the daily *La Jornada* and W Radio, according to local media reports.

The voices of the men heard on the tape discussed plans to imprison Cacho and rape her in jail. Cacho had previously exposed a child pornography and prostitution ring involving government officials. In 2008, in western Mexico, two unidentified men beat and stabbed the deputy director of a local daily, Luis Pablo Guardado Negrete, who survived, while questioning him about a story on a sexual assault scandal at a local gym.

Of course, not all rape victims are women, as noted in a CNN report on James Landrith, a former Marine based at Camp Lejeune in North Carolina, who has spoken out about his own rape and on behalf of other sexual assault victims, in particular men victimized by women. According to a 2010 report by the U.S. Centers for Disease Control and Prevention, nearly 1 in 5 women and 1 in 71 men in the United States have been raped. The actual number is most likely higher, experts say, as sexual violence is severely underreported in the United States as elsewhere, particularly among male victims.

Rape is also used as a tool of war. A World Bank study published in 2011 found that 48 women are raped every hour in the Democratic Republic of Congo, based on data collected in 2007. Many of the rapists are members of different armed forces. Many women and men have been reported raped in Syria since its civil war began in 2011. Government and allied militia forces committed more than three-fourths of the sexual attacks tracked by the Women Under Siege Project, which has documented many rapes and other crimes that were not otherwise reported in the press.

CPJ has also covered journalists who themselves were sexually assaulted or raped, most notably the widely publicized case of CBS television correspondent and CPJ board member Lara Logan who was attacked while she was covering an anti-government demonstration in Cairo's Tahrir Square in 2011.

In many other cases, sexual assaults are kept quiet because they occur within the home. Elisa Lees Muñoz is the executive director of the International Women's Media Foundation, a Washington-based group that works with some of the world's top female journalists. Muñoz said in an interview that a surprising number of the journalists from various regions, including the Middle East, are themselves victims of domestic violence. Yet this is one story that none of them will report or discuss in public.

"These are well-educated women who have a voice in their own societies," Muñoz told CPJ. "Yet they won't tell their own stories, so how could they tell others?"

These women are hardly alone.

"People are raped by their own husbands, and no one wants to talk about that," said Beatrice Nas of Uganda. Even in cases that do not involve domestic violence, she said, the perpetrators are still people "usually known in the community."

Journalists who have experience covering sexual violence counsel colleagues to respect the wishes and interests of victims, so as not to worsen their situation. "We leave it up to her," said Chanam, referring to female victims of sexual violence.

**Frank Smyth** *is CPJ's senior adviser for journalist security. He has reported on armed conflicts, organized crime, and human rights from nations including El Salvador, Guatemala, Colombia, Cuba, Rwanda, Uganda, Eritrea, Ethiopia, Sudan, Jordan, and Iraq.*

# Afghan Journalists Steadfast as International Withdrawal Approaches

## By Bob Dietz

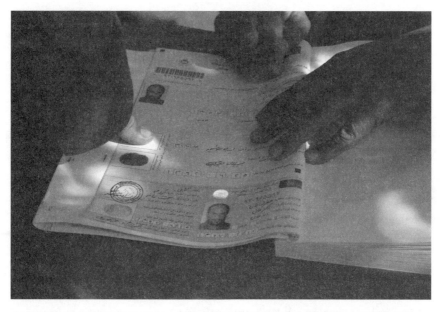

An Afghan man marks his application for voter registration in Kabul, Afghanistan, on September 16, 2013. The future of the nation's journalists may hinge on the presidential election scheduled for April 2014.

*Source:* AP/Rahmat Gul.

Local journalists in Afghanistan face mounting threats in 2014 as the country braces for a withdrawal of foreign troops, rapidly diminishing international aid, and a contentious presidential election. Yet many local reporters are upbeat, their optimism reflecting a sense of determination to build on the progress that has been achieved.

Reporting news in Afghanistan requires navigating not only officials in government, the military, and the security apparatus, but also traditional regional and ethnic power brokers who seek a return to power; illegal, armed groups, including local militias; and vigilantes and criminal gangs supporting themselves through extortion, kidnapping, and trafficking in weapons and drugs. Just about all players on the country's political stage are responsible for attacks and harassment of journalists—from the villages and regional centers to Kabul, the capital.

Most of the factions and armies carry out daily attacks against one another across the country, with civilians targeted in terrorist attacks or caught in crossfire or drone strikes. There is relative stability in the major cities, but many of the roads linking them are shooting galleries for insurgents and bountiful hunting grounds for kidnappers and hijackers.

There is no single insurgency in Afghanistan. In the background, regional political leaders—Afghans readily refer to them as "warlords"—are maneuvering for power, stockpiling weapons and building up war chests. Ethnically aligned groups in the north and west are re-arming with help from neighboring countries. To the south and east, some factions of the Taliban seem prepared to talk peace, but others continue to battle. For years the Taliban have been divided into Afghan and Pakistani groups, often at odds, and, within each, factions with varying loyalties.

"When I speak with diplomats, they agree that it is impossible to predict what will come next in Afghanistan," said Ahmed Rashid, one of the region's best known and widely read correspondents and a member of the board of directors of the Committee to Protect Journalists.

How dire a situation journalists face may hinge mostly on the scheduled presidential election on April 5, 2014, to replace Hamid Karzai, who is serving his second and last term as president. Many of the candidates are the warlords Afghans speak so openly about. If all goes as planned, the voting will bring Afghanistan's first transition from one elected leader to another.

While the NATO countries focus on what roles the International Security Assistance Force (ISAF) will play after 2014, Afghanistan's chances for survival as a democracy of any sort will be determined more by the electoral process than by troop numbers. Success will depend on whether the election is perceived as legitimate and whether the next president will have the skills to rule with the conciliatory political savvy necessary to stave off open conflict.

The predictions range from tentative stability after the voting to a quick return to the all-out civil war that followed the collapse of the communist Najibullah-regime in 1992.

"Almost everyone who has gained something in the last 10 years is worried about losing it," Lotfullah Najafizada, head of current affairs at Tolo TV, the country's largest independent broadcaster, told CPJ in Kabul.

As an Afghan who refused to flee his homeland, Najafizada has a vested interest in peace. "This society has grown enough not to see all these gains vanish overnight," Najafizada said. "Some gains are irreversible. Post-2014, violence could get worse, but even if we saw the return of the Taliban it would not be a repeat of the dark regime. Media and press freedom would not go back to point zero."

Point zero was pre-9/11 Afghanistan, under Taliban rule, a country with one government radio station, Voice of Sharia, used mainly to broadcast official edicts and religious pronouncements. There was no television, no independent media. For years, Afghans relied on short-wave radio broadcasts or bootlegged satellite feeds to tune in to a wide range of foreign broadcasters including the BBC and Voice of America for information.

A decade later, the Center for International Media Assistance at the National Endowment for Democracy could report on "an explosion of news" taking place in Afghanistan.

It counted 175 FM radio stations, 75 TV channels, four news agencies, and hundreds of publications, including seven daily newspapers, Internet cafes in major cities, and mobile phones in the hands of about half the population of 29 million people.

"Afghanistan's main cities are close to media saturation—Kabul has 30 TV channels and 42 radio stations, and the smaller cities have 10 to 25 TV channels and approximately 20 radio stations each," the report said.

Now, local journalists are gauging an anticipated drawdown by their own employers. Some Afghan publications and broadcasters almost certainly face cuts in aid programs, while international news organizations are expected to reduce staffing and expenditures just as they did when U.S. troops withdrew from Iraq.

■ ■ ■

CPJ commissioned a telephone survey of 15 Afghan journalists in five of the country's main cities—Kabul, Kandahar, Mazr-i-Sharif, Herat, and Jalalabad—to determine how they viewed the future. We promised anonymity in exchange for frankness about the media outlook in their country. Their evaluations were mixed, but we found a surprisingly positive outlook, especially on the part of men. Some of the respondents worked only for Afghan media; others had a mix of foreign and local employers.

In Kandahar, the Taliban heartland, where despite shrinking numbers journalists enjoy a considerable degree of professional organization and group identity, a TV reporter told us that, though Taliban threats are a problem, in the end "we will have a smooth transition." He said the withdrawal of foreign troops and reduction in aid from international donors might have an economic impact on all businesses, but that his local television channel was likely to remain in operation.

Over all, the number of journalists in the area has gone down, the TV reporter said, "especially people working for international media." But, he added, "I am personally optimistic for 2014."

In neighboring Zabul province, a reporter for an Afghan news agency said the government is a bigger problem for journalists than the Taliban, a view echoed by many others. The reporter said he was once detained in 2011 for reporting on government officials seeking bribes from civilians.

"I was first threatened and later detained by some of the officials close to the person I wrote about," the reporter told us. "I should admit that the Taliban so far have not threatened us because of our journalistic work but rather they are very quick in responding to our questions and inquiries when something happens. However, they do emphasize that they want us to write about their side of the story."

Far to the north, in relatively stable Balkh province, the woman who heads a radio station there said she and her predominantly female staff faced a range of problems, but troop withdrawals were not high on her list. "The big problem in our media is the lack of training in professional journalism and finding good jobs," she said.

"Over all it is difficult to be a journalist in Afghanistan, but being a female journalist in Afghanistan is even more dangerous," she said. "Women are constantly harassed and threatened by officials, unknown people, and some family members, so it makes it difficult for girls to work in the field of media—even though it is very important that we have female reporters to reflect the many challenges that Afghan women face in this country."

War or no war, women journalists in Afghanistan add another level of concern and complexity when it comes to safety. In an interview with CPJ in Kabul in July 2013, Shafiqa Habibi, director of the Afghan Women Journalist Union, estimated that of 2,300 women journalists, about 300 had stopped working recently because of concerns for their personal security.

In addition to direct threats from religious militants, many women face intense family pressure to stop working. Family elders want the women to reduce their public profile either because they feel such prominence is unseemly or because they fear repercussions for the broader family or from militants. Habibi said the trend is accelerating.

■ ■ ■

In general, few of the journalists CPJ surveyed seemed on the verge of quitting their profession because of the looming political and military transition, even if the country grows more violent. Battle-hardened, they do not appear ready to cut and run.

In 2012, Afghanistan was the world's greatest source of refugees, with some 2.6 million, according to the latest figures available from the United Nations High Commissioner for Refugees (UNHCR), the U.N. refugee agency, down from slightly more than three million in 2011. But CPJ has seen no corresponding uptick in Afghan journalists leaving the country. In recent years, the number of such cases received by CPJ's Journalist Assistance program, often but not always including requests for asylum, remains below 10 per year.

Should post-election events reach crisis proportions, some local reporters may make plans to leave their towns for the relative safety of Kabul, which, with an estimated population of more than 3 million, is large enough to keep people discreetly out of view.

Others, particularly Afghan journalists working for international media, may cross the border into Pakistan or other neighboring countries, while some may seek to leave the region entirely. Many foreign employers, but by no means all, accept some level of responsibility for helping move local employees under threat.

In three to six months, dangerous situations in most countries have usually ameliorated enough to allow people to return home, CPJ research shows. And although it might seem an ideal solution, seeking asylum is a difficult and often painful path for endangered journalists.

CPJ urges journalists at risk to find sanctuary in their own country if at all possible. The organization has seen many talented men and women leave their countries to escape dangerous situations and flounder. Their expertise, so priceless in their own society, is often not valued elsewhere. And worse, back home their country is deprived of their intellectual resources, a brain drain that developing societies, including Afghanistan, can ill afford.

In peace, as in war, what is obvious is that without local journalists, media companies would be hard pressed to gather news. In 2010, CPJ predicted: "We can expect to see ground-level news gathering handed off to trusted local Afghan reporters, those who have proven to have the skill, reliability, and the bravery to go where foreign news agencies will no longer be willing to risk their foreign staff reporters' safety." To a large extent that has become true. While the 2014 endgame might bring about a temporary influx of outside media, it will be mostly Afghan reporters in the field covering the news in the long run.

*Livia Rurarz-Huygens contributed reporting to this essay.*

*Bob Dietz, coordinator of CPJ's Asia Program, has reported across the continent for news outlets such as CNN and Asiaweek. He has led numerous CPJ missions, including ones to Afghanistan, Pakistan, the Philippines, and Sri Lanka.*

# 4

# MEDIA AND MONEY

# Journalists in Hong Kong and Taiwan Battle Beijing's Influence

*By a CPJ Contributor*

**Protesters like this one in Taipei on September 1, 2012, have helped derail plans for consolidation in Taiwan's media industry. Her slogan reads, "You Are So Huge. I Am Not Afraid."**

*Source:* AP/Chiang Ying-ying.

"Self-censorship—it's like the plague, a cancerous growth, multiplying on a daily basis," former journalist and current Hong Kong legislator Claudia Mo said. "In Hong Kong, media organizations are mostly owned by tycoons with business interests in China. They don't want to lose advertising revenue from Chinese companies and they don't want to anger the central government."

That should not be surprising. More than half of Hong Kong media owners have accepted appointments to the main political assemblies of China—the National People's Congress (NPC) and the Chinese People's Political Consultative Conference (CPPCC). Recent appointments to one of the two assemblies include Charles Ho of the Sing Tao news group, Richard Li of Now TV and the *Hong Kong Economic Journal*, and Peter Woo of i-Cable television. Journalists and academics say they are concerned that the city's media leaders are being absorbed into China's political elite.

Adding to concerns in the territory is a series of physical attacks on journalists, as well as steps taken by the local legislature that would hamper reporting.

Meanwhile, in Taiwan, many media owners have close business ties to Beijing, which they are loath to jeopardize by drawing disfavor on the mainland. The Taiwanese press is also vulnerable to financial intervention in the form of advertising by Chinese interests—including some ads disguised as news, journalists say.

The state of media freedom in Hong Kong and Taiwan is significant in part because news outlets in both places have in the past provided comprehensive, independent coverage of China, filling a gap left by the tightly restricted mainland press. Any rise in interference, including self-censorship, would imperil the ability of the Hong Kong and Taiwanese press to play a watchdog role.

When Hong Kong returned to Chinese control from British rule in 1997, the territory was granted a high degree of autonomy to manage its domestic affairs under a "one country, two systems" framework. Socialism as practiced by the People's Republic of China would not be extended to Hong Kong for at least 50 years, and the rights of its residents—including freedom of speech, freedom of the press, and freedom of assembly—were to be protected under the

Basic Law, worked out between London and Beijing. The Basic Law was to be essentially Hong Kong's constitution.

Nearly 17 years on, Hong Kong's media freedom is at a low point. A public opinion survey by the University of Hong Kong in 2013 found that more than half of the public believes the local press practices self-censorship. The United Nations has signaled concern, urging the Hong Kong government in a March 2013 meeting of the U.N. Human Rights Committee to "take vigorous measures to repeal any unreasonable direct or indirect restrictions on freedom of expression, in particular for the media and academia, to take effective steps including investigation of attacks on journalists, and to implement the right of access to information by public bodies."

According to a survey of journalists by the Hong Kong Journalists Association (HKJA) in 2012, the most pervasive problems facing Hong Kong media are self-censorship and a rising number of physical attacks and threats against journalists. Of the survey's 663 respondents, nearly 40 percent said they or their supervisors had recently played down information unfavorable to China's central government, advertisers, media owners, or the local government. The HKJA has been tracking censorship trends in Hong Kong since 1968.

Compounding the issue of self-censorship, the central government has sometimes put direct pressure on Hong Kong media. In the past, Beijing had relied on discreet ways to carry messages to Hong Kong media owners, such as asking middlemen to speak with newspaper editors. It was rare to hear of Chinese officials contacting editors and journalists directly, said Shirley Yam, HKJA's vice-chairwoman. "Now the gloves are off," she said in an interview.

Yam and legislator Claudia Mo both told CPJ they believe that Beijing's meddling in media coverage of Hong Kong's 2012 election for chief executive was a turning point. During the campaign to elect Hong Kong's current leader, Leung Chun-ying, the propaganda chief of China's representative agency in Hong Kong, the Liaison Office, called the owner of the daily *Hong Kong Economic Journal* to complain about the newspaper's critical coverage of Leung, according to news reports. "That's something that we have never heard of before, and people were shocked," Yam said. Although the daily's owner, Richard

Li, is not outwardly pro-Beijing, his father, Li Ka-shing, is one of the most influential businessmen in China and one of the richest men in Asia. Both father and son are members of the CPPCC.

Three reporters at the *Journal* told CPJ that since the Liaison Office's phone call, they were being ordered by their supervisors to write fewer critical reports about Hong Kong's leader and to back up any negative statements about Leung or his government—even in opinion pieces—with substantive supporting evidence. *Journal* executive editor Tim Chan did not respond to CPJ's emailed request for comment.

One reporter at the *Journal* said journalists in Hong Kong are getting used to self-censorship and heavy pressure from Beijing. "There is really no such thing as 'independent-minded' media or media that aims for neutrality in Hong Kong anymore," he told CPJ. "It's not that journalists are giving up on their ethics. Often, self-censorship happens when journalists realize that editors won't accept certain kinds of 'sensitive' story ideas and they learn where the lines are drawn. China's influence is just too powerful. You either accept the status quo or you quit." Like most of the journalists who spoke with CPJ, the reporter requested anonymity, citing risk of professional repercussions.

Also during the 2012 election campaign, the pro-Beijing *Sing Pao* newspaper twisted an opinion piece by commentator Johnny Lau so much that it ended up saying the opposite of what he had intended. Lau had lambasted both Leung and his leading opponent, Henry Tang, but his editors "changed my column in 11 places, making me seem like a supporter of Leung when I had clearly written that I supported neither candidate," Lau told CPJ. The chief editor of *Sing Pao* initially apologized, but one month later discontinued Lau's column after he wrote about the death of a prominent Chinese democracy advocate.

"It is obvious that self-censorship in Hong Kong has gotten much worse across all forms of media since the handover," said Lau, who has worked as an editor and commentator in Hong Kong for more than 40 years. "Beijing influences media in effective ways, such as by threatening to pull advertising, harming the business interests of media owners in China, and tightening the release of information."

The founder of Next Media Limited, Jimmy Lai, said his publications have endured a boycott by China-based advertisers since 2003. Next publishes the critical, widely circulated Chinese-language *Apple*

*Daily* as well as newsmagazines in Hong Kong and Taiwan. "China is a huge market, so if you please China as a media owner you think you will get benefits in the world's largest market," Lai told CPJ via email. "The funny thing is that I really can't think of one pro-China media owner in Hong Kong who has really benefited by trying to please China. They think they can play a game with the Communists, but that is not how it works. Once they get you, they own you."

Lai said that Next, the largest publicly listed media company in Hong Kong, has been able to live without the advertising, "but it kills any media start-up that is not willing to toe the pro-China line," he said.

■ ■ ■

In recent years, the majority of Hong Kong news media have fallen into opposing camps of pro- or anti-Beijing. Much of the Chinese-language press depends on lurid crime and celebrity coverage to boost sales. Others focus solely on business news. For English media, which serve the local English-speaking population as well as international readers, the *South China Morning Post* and *The Standard* used to compete fiercely as the leading newspapers. Now, only a handful of international media maintain bureaus in Hong Kong to cover the city, while *The Standard* was cut down to a slim, free daily in 2007. This left the *Post* with a virtual monopoly on English media covering Hong Kong.

In broadcast, meanwhile, Beijing exerts an even stronger influence because the high cost of news operations is prohibitive to independent media, according to Lau. The government also tightly controls broadcast licenses, and can reject applications without providing a reason.

A journalist at Television Broadcasts Limited (TVB), which was until recently one of only two free-to-air television broadcasters in Hong Kong, told CPJ that it is difficult for staff at TVB to challenge signs that the station's managers voluntarily censor coverage. "Our station has received complaints from the public in the past for appearing to be pro-government, but it is hard to prove that there is actual censorship," she said. "For example, if a documentary on a sensitive political issue is pulled, the managers won't be so blunt about their reasoning. They may tell producers that their work was biased because they did not seek views of pro-Beijing loyalists."

John Berthelson, the editor of the independent news website *Asia Sentinel*, which monitors press freedom issues in Hong Kong with the help of anonymous tips from journalists, told CPJ that Hong Kong journalists want foreign observers to understand that "freedom of the press in the city is obviously in danger at a time when it is really important. Hong Kong is at a critical juncture. Its relations with the mainland are fraught. There seems to be significant antagonism to the mainland among Hong Kong citizens and Leung," he said, and the central government "would like to see things quiet down."

Nowhere have issues of self-censorship been more pointed than at the *South China Morning Post*, which has had a series of chief editors since Rupert Murdoch's News Corporation sold it to Chinese-Malaysian tycoon Robert Kuok in 1993. Kuok has a controlling interest in Shangri-La luxury hotels and other large holdings in China. One of Asia's richest people, Kuok was selected as one of Beijing's advisers on Hong Kong's future in the run-up to the 1997 handover. He has been accused by Hong Kong media commentators of being pro-establishment and of forcing the departures of a string of *Post* editors and reporters critical of Beijing, accusations he has denied. But, for example, in 2000 he publicly denounced former China editor Willy Lam for "exaggeration and fabrication." Lam resigned soon after and now teaches Chinese studies at the Chinese University of Hong Kong. Lam told CPJ that Kuok made early investments in China and has personal relationships with some top leaders, including former Premier Zhu Rongji. "Of course he didn't want me to write anything that would embarrass China," Lam said.

Under Wang Xiangwei, who was appointed in January 2012 and is the first mainland-born chief editor, the newspaper has again courted controversy. Tensions played out in dramatic fashion in June 2012 when senior copy editor Alex Price questioned why Wang had reduced a prominent breaking story on the death of Tiananmen dissident Li Wangyang to a news brief in the back pages. "It looks an awful lot like self-censorship," Price wrote in an email. Wang replied: "I don't have to explain to you anything. I made the decision and I stand by it. If you don't like it, you know what to do," according to leaked emails published in the press.

Subsequently, 25,000 people took to Hong Kong's streets to demand a thorough investigation into Li Wangyang's death, which had been ruled a suicide. Most Hong Kong newspapers featured his death on their front pages, and the *Post* followed suit with several strong articles and commentaries, some of which were written by Wang. But it wasn't enough to deflect accusations from the wider public and international media about self-censorship. Pro-democracy activists burned newspapers outside the *Post*'s office, and editorial staff members signed a petition voicing concern about the paper's credibility. Twenty-three former *Post* journalists wrote an open letter to a *Post* executive, stating, "The constant changes in the editorship of the *Post* suggest that either the owners do not know what they want, or they want something that no credible senior journalists will provide." Price told CPJ that he wrote the email to Wang knowing he would likely lose his job as a consequence. Three months later the *Post* declined to renew his contract.

In an emailed response to staff concerns, which Wang also sent to the *Asia Sentinel*, Wang addressed his exchange with Price, saying: "This matter should have been resolved in a much more constructive way." He added: "I want to make it absolutely clear that I did not try to downplay the Li Wangyang story. . . . Although I chose not to prioritize coverage on the first day it broke until more facts and details surrounding the circumstances of this case could be established, we subsequently splashed no less than three front pages, two leaders, plus several other prominent positions including two articles by myself."

Paul Mooney, who was an award-winning, Beijing-based contributor to the *Post* for 20 years, said, "The problem is that people on the outside can't tell what's being censored on the inside." He told CPJ, "What outsiders can't see is what is being ignored, spiked or rewritten in order to play down" critical stories. Mooney built his career on investigative and human rights reporting but during the last nine months of his employment, he had only two news stories in the newspaper, and one of them was about pandas. "I don't believe the China editors rejected all my story ideas. I think [Wang] Xiangwei told them not to take anything from me," he said. The *Post* discontinued his employment contract in May 2012.

■ ■ ■

Meanwhile, the HKJA has recorded several violent attacks on journalists, which were once rare in Hong Kong. One attack targeted Next

Media on June 30, 2013, when three masked men threatened distribution workers with knives and burned 26,000 copies of *Apple Daily*, according to news reports.

Earlier the same month, in an attack relating to another media company, *iSun Affairs* publisher Chen Ping was beaten by a group of unidentified baton-wielding men. The Hong Kong-based magazine is known for outspoken reporting on sensitive mainland issues.

Next's owner Lai is blunt regarding who he believes is behind the attacks. "The Hong Kong police have tried to solve these attacks and they do send a number of patrols by our home and businesses. But Hong Kong can't chase people into China, and that is where these attacks come from," he told CPJ. "Don't worry," he added, "they don't bother me."

The attacks came against a backdrop of restrictive legal measures. The Hong Kong government has proposed or passed laws that threaten to undermine the nuts and bolts of newsgathering—and has failed to pass laws that would broaden public access to information. Journalists in the city have long called for a freedom of information law and an archiving of information law. Hong Kong does have access rules, but because the government is not required to keep old records and can refuse to disclose any information it deems sensitive, the rules are meaningless, according to Doreen Weisenhaus, associate professor of media law and ethics at the University of Hong Kong and the author of the book *Hong Kong Media Law: A Guide for Journalists and Media Professionals*. Government officials can simply tell journalists that records have been destroyed or that certain information cannot be disclosed, without providing a reason, she said.

Provisions of the city's privacy law that went into effect in April 2013 could subject journalists to five years in jail or fines up to 1 million Hong Kong dollars (US$129,000) if they reveal information that "causes psychological harm" or "causes loss." The law also gives targets of investigative reporting the right to "request to access personal data" collected by journalists. Journalists may mount a defense that they "reasonably believed" they were reporting in the public interest, but that aspect of the law is vague and undefined. When asked to clarify the definition of public interest, Privacy Commissioner for Personal Data

Allan Chiang told CPJ "it is up to judges to review complaints on a case-by-case basis."

City legislators also proposed to introduce a bill to outlaw stalking, which if implemented, could be used as a tool to block journalists from waiting in public spaces to pursue interviews. "With the proposed law, journalists can be seen as a nuisance. If they go to a spot, the target of their news story can call the police and the journalists would be shooed away," Weisenhaus said. "Hong Kong has clung onto a lot of old laws inherited from the U.K., from court reporting restrictions to contempt of court, defamation and so forth," while other former colonies have moved on.

■ ■ ■

In Taiwan, journalists say they experience pressure from China in ways both similar and different than their Hong Kong colleagues. Most reporters CPJ interviewed in Taiwan also requested anonymity because of concerns over job security.

As in Hong Kong, most Taiwanese media are backed by individuals who own an array of businesses. News outlets in Taiwan have long been divided along clear political lines. Some are in open support of the Kuomintang (KMT), which favors greater integration with China. Others back the Democratic Progressive Party (DPP), which is staunchly pro-independence.

Journalists say that media owners on both sides are undermining the country's freewheeling press in order to protect their expanding business interests on the mainland. Broadcast outlets in particular have come under fire recently as pro-China tycoons have sought to monopolize the airwaves. But unlike in Hong Kong, broadcast media are no longer subject to licensing and programming reviews by the government.

"Like in Hong Kong, the tycoon bosses of Taiwan media are increasingly pushing their media companies to flatter Beijing because they do business with China," said Chen Hsiao-yi, chairwoman of the Association of Taiwan Journalists and a reporter at the Chinese language *Liberty Times* for 16 years. "Taiwan media are also becoming more and more reliant on Chinese advertising. They are self-censoring for mostly financial and not political reasons," she told CPJ.

Michael Cole, deputy news editor of the *Taipei Times*, a pro-independence English-language newspaper, told CPJ: "As a rule of thumb, news media that stay away from criticizing China will attract more advertisement revenue. Over time, this can gradually elbow out news organizations that are critical of China."

A journalist at Taiwan's Central News Agency, the official state news agency, which is 50 percent owned by the Taiwanese government, said interference comes from the local government as well. "We are not a mouthpiece, but no matter which party is in power the government will have some sort of influence on us," she told CPJ. "Some politically sensitive stories require a final clearance from our editor-in-chief before we can publish them."

A reporter at the *China Post*, another English-language newspaper, told CPJ, "Many of my [fellow journalists] complain that their bosses would often receive calls from higher ranking Taiwanese government officials, persuading them not to write or print something."

Journalists also warn that Beijing could be circumventing Taiwan government regulations meant to prevent the mainland from influencing local media. Under legally binding guidelines set in 1993, Chinese news companies require Taiwanese government permission to enter Taiwan's market. In April 2011, the *China Post*, which is historically supportive of the Kuomintang, reprinted seven articles originally published in official Chinese state media. The *Post* did not mention the origin of the pieces. The newspaper responded to criticism that it circumvented the 1993 guidelines by saying that the content had come from the Asia News Network, a content-sharing partnership with headquarters in Bangkok. *China Daily*, a Chinese government-owned English newspaper, is a member of the network.

Journalists are also concerned about growing investment in Taiwan media coming from Hong Kong. The city is exempt from regulations barring China from investing in local media. The onus falls on Taiwan's regulators to monitor investments and news products coming from Hong Kong and elsewhere to ensure there are no mainland China influences.

"Whether or not the regulators are successfully doing this is highly questionable," said Cole of the *Taipei Times*. "The government in Taiwan conveniently looks the other way when influential individuals engage in dealings with China. There have been many confirmed cases of a newspaper accepting cash from Beijing to run disguised advertising and one-sided articles in favor of China. And although regulators caught on, asking a multibillionaire media owner to pay a fine isn't exactly an effective means of deterrence."

Cole was referring to tycoon Tsai Eng-meng, who purchased the China Times Group, a Taiwanese media conglomerate, in 2008. Tsai made his fortune selling snack foods and beverages, operating more than 100 manufacturing plants in China. *Forbes* listed him as Taiwan's richest man in 2013.

The group's flagship newspaper, the *China Times*, has been repeatedly fined by regulators for disguising advertising purchased by Beijing as news reports, and is regularly criticized for one-sided reporting in favor of China. The problem of "embedded marketing" came to public attention in late 2010 when veteran *China Times* reporter Dennis Huang resigned in protest, leading to a public campaign to end the practice. In 2011, Taiwan lawmakers amended legislation to prohibit Taiwanese government agencies from using public funds for "paid news," but the amendment did not apply to foreign governments, meaning that the legislation did nothing to strengthen safeguards against interference from Beijing. Taiwan's main media regulatory body, the National Communications Commission, did not respond to CPJ's requests for comment.

The *China Times* was again hit with controversy in 2012 when an undercover investigation by the Association of Taiwan Journalists discovered that the paper had been paid by a press officer in China to cover a visit by Su Shulin, governor of Fujian Province, according to strict guidelines laid down by the mainland.

One journalist said Tsai stands out for his close ties with Beijing and the "wacky" examples of "extreme self-censorship" in the *China Times*. "I honestly don't think that Tsai will succeed in manipulating Taiwanese opinions," said the journalist, who works at *China Post*. "Taiwanese people are not that stupid. They won't be brainwashed by his reports." (The *China Post*, an English newspaper, is neither related to nor a direct competitor to the *China Times*.)

Early in 2013, Tsai made moves to take control of the country's largest newspaper, Next Media's *Apple Daily*. More than 100,000 protesters rallied to oppose the purchase, and popular outrage effectively derailed the plan.

But Tsai continues to expand his media empire. In July 2012, after an 18-month deliberation, regulators gave approval for his company, Want Want Holdings, to purchase the cable-television operator China Network Systems, one of Taiwan's largest cable television providers. Critics expressed alarm at the decision. The *Taipei Times* wrote in a February 2013 editorial that the purchase has "effectively granted control over about one-third of the nation's media market, including 23 percent of all cable subscribers," to Tsai.

■ ■ ■

Given Beijing's goal of unification with Taiwan, many commentators have argued that Beijing has upheld the "one country, two systems" framework in Hong Kong in part to demonstrate to Taiwan that it would enjoy a level of freedom upon unification. Lin Cho-shui, a former DPP legislator, wrote in the *Taipei Times* in 2012 that Beijing's plan has backfired. He cited the reception in Hong Kong of Hu Jintao, then China's president, in July 2012 as an example of Hong Kong dissatisfaction with Chinese rule. "Just as Hu was making his speech, someone in the hall shouted demands for the vindication of the protagonists from the 1989 Tiananmen Square democracy uprising and an end to one-party rule in China, while crowds of people protested outside the venue. In the evening there was a protest which 100,000 people joined," Lin wrote. People in Hong Kong have long called on Beijing to reassess its condemnation of the 1989 protests in Tiananmen Square, which culminated in the June 4 military crackdown that killed as many as several thousand civilians.

During Hu's visit, Hong Kong journalists also showed that they would fight for press freedom and freedom of expression in the territory. Hu was touring a cruise ship terminal when an *Apple Daily* reporter shouted a question to him. "President Hu, have you heard that Hong Kong people hope to reverse the verdict of June 4?" reporter Hon Yiu-ting asked. "Have you heard?" Hon was immediately detained by security officers and held for 15 minutes, but other reporters continued to shout questions at Hu, and then surrounded a police officer to demand why their colleague had been detained.

■ ■ ■

With the mainstream media increasingly compromised, some journalists in Hong Kong and Taiwan are pinning hope on the development of independent online news outlets. Unlike on the mainland, government censors do not control expression on the Internet in Hong Kong or Taiwan. Lin Yuting, a former reporter at Taiwan's *China Post*, said that before he left the newspaper in 2012, he saw more influence in the form of advertorials by Chinese companies and a weekly lifestyle insert provided by mainland Chinese media. "At the same time, I've seen a refreshing growth of online forums and activism websites in Taiwan," he told CPJ.

Lam, the professor and former *South China Morning Post* China editor, agrees that online media can provide an alternative to mainstream media organizations, which are bound to become more heavily censored. "Beijing must be quite happy. At this point in Hong Kong at least, Beijing has already gotten what they wanted. All the mainstream media are self-censoring. Only Next Media is holding out," he said. "But the situation is not that bleak because of the emergence of online media outlets."

In a sign that the public is prepared to pressure the government to improve media freedom in Hong Kong, tens of thousands of protesters demonstrated for weeks in the autumn of 2013, after the government rejected a free-to-air television license for the Hong Kong Television Network. HKTV is a startup that promised to broadcast critical programming. The government's refusal to provide reasons for the license rejection raised suspicions that the influence of Beijing was behind the decision. Protesters waved banners and shared messages over social media, demanding that they wanted "a fair system, not a black box system" or a "monopolistic" system. Others expressed fear that the closed-door licensing process foreshadows what is in store for the city's future elections.

Hong Kong will elect its next leader in 2017 in what Beijing had promised would be the first election conducted by universal suffrage, in which each citizen will have a vote. But already, Beijing has ruled out open nominations for chief executive candidates, meaning the candidates will be selected instead by a committee stacked with Beijing supporters.

"Tensions will continue to build up, and it is critical that journalism in Hong Kong remains robust in the run-up to the 2017 election—and international media needs to pay close attention, too," said Sham Yee-lan, chairwoman of the Hong Kong Journalists Association. "Otherwise, how can the public know what they're up against?"

*The author chooses not to be identified to avoid professional repercussions.*

# Advertising and Censorship in East Africa's Press

*By Tom Rhodes*

Kenyans read election coverage in the Mathare slum in Nairobi, the capital, on March 9, 2013. One reason that advertising revenue trumps circulation for East Africa's newspapers is that readers often share papers to save money.

*Source:* Reuters/Goran Tomasevic.

M any newspapers in East Africa are thriving—some fat with ads, enjoying solid circulation and little competition—but there is broad concern that all that advertising is also promoting self-censorship and corrupting news coverage.

While newspapers elsewhere in the world shrivel, thanks to shrinking ad revenue and online competition, they are still dominant in much of East Africa, where a growing middle class and prohibitively expensive online browsing have allowed the printed word to survive and even thrive.

A prominent example of this success is the Nation Media Group, the largest independent media house in East and Central Africa and publisher of Kenya's principal daily newspaper, the *Daily Nation*. The group increased its revenue by nearly 50 percent in five years to 12.347 billion Kenyan shillings (US$142.5 million) in 2012.

Newspapers account for the bulk of that revenue. Paralleling that trajectory, the advertising market in Kenya rose nearly fivefold in the past five years, while there were smaller gains in Uganda and Tanzania, according to Joe Otim, media research and monitoring director at Ipsos research company.

"In East Africa, the advertiser is king," said veteran Kenyan journalist John Gatchie, who works as a media consultant in the region.

Because they represent the greatest source of revenue, advertisers—especially governments and government-owned enterprises—wield huge influence, which often allows them to quietly control what is published and what is not, according to journalists and media analysts. Advertisers offer lucrative ads to sweeten any coverage or threaten to stop ads if a paper writes critically about them.

This type of back-door soft censorship, generally invisible to the public, is not a problem unique to East Africa. In West Africa, state-owned newspapers lead in most markets except Nigeria, since they receive the lion's share of government advertisement revenue, said Sulemana Braimah, deputy director of the press freedom group Media Foundation for West Africa. In southern Africa, advertisements are sometimes used by politicians to discourage critical coverage, said Raymond Louw, former editor and publisher and veteran media freedom campaigner in South Africa. And the issue surfaces in other regions of the world, perhaps most dramatically in Turkey in 2013 during the Gezi

Park protests in Istanbul. Media owners there, beholden to the government, suppressed coverage of the demonstrations by their own reporters, some of whom they subsequently fired at the government's behest.

Such practices are also notable in Latin America, where government advertising has been widely used for decades as a cudgel to punish media critics or as a reward to bolster supporters. In a survey of 1,000 Argentine journalists in 2011, for example, dependence on government advertising was ranked the third most serious challenge facing the Argentine media after low salaries and lack of professionalism. Polling results showed that 58 percent of the subjects thought journalism in the country was "conditioned" and 72 percent said they thought the business departments at their outlets had influence in the newsroom.

■ ■ ■

In East Africa, advertisers are a mixed blessing, said Deodatus Balile, managing editor of the Tanzanian private weekly *Jamhuri*. "Advertisers are the biggest financial supporters of the press and yet they are also the biggest suppressors of freedom of the press," he said.

One novel news suppression technique adopted in Tanzania is a blanket advertising strategy that involves placing full-page ads that leave no room for anything else on the front and back pages, according to John Mireny, publications and research manager of the Media Council of Tanzania, an independent regulator. The ruling Chama Cha Mapinduzi Party ("Party of the Revolution") did just that with all of Tanzania's newspapers in 2010, stifling coverage of the opposition party's inaugural campaign rally, Mireny said.

In Tanzania, ad revenue covers about 85 percent of a newspaper's running costs, according to Balile, which provides little margin for aggressive reporting that might alienate clients. Despite a relatively high literacy rate, circulation levels are low, in part because readers in Tanzania share newspapers to save money.

Newspapers in impoverished South Sudan, a country that gained independence in 2011 after decades of civil war, are struggling. "The market is narrow and distribution is poor," said Badru Mulumba, editor of the *New Times*. "With such poor sales, any advertiser is viewed with respect and welcomed with roses."

In 2012, the press in Uganda was awash with stories alleging graft in the prime minister's office involving misappropriated donor funds. "As editors we insisted on covering the story despite some objections," said Barbara Among, foreign editor of Uganda's leading independent *Daily Monitor*.

But the office of the prime minister, which oversees five ministries, also happens to be one of the biggest advertisers in Uganda. After the government placed numerous ads in the press, fewer graft stories were published, local journalists said. "Now with the prime minister's office's big budget, there is less reporting on the scandal," said Don Wanyama, the *Daily Monitor*'s managing editor. "The press could have done a lot more in terms of digging up the rot in that office, but fears of lost ad revenue silenced everyone."

Influencing the press using the financial clout of ad placements is not only a government affair. In September, an electric company with indirect links to the government in Tanzania informed the private daily *Raia Mwema* (Good Citizen) that a cell-phone company had been illegally connected to its power lines and owed billions of Tanzanian shillings.

"Imagine, only one newspaper published the story but kept it very vague without saying the name of the cell-phone company," Mbaraka Islam, the newspaper's news director, said.

"Very few can write about cell-phone companies such as Vodacom, Airtel, Tigo—they have financial muscle," Balile said. "If you write negatively about them, they go straight to the courts, acquire a court injunction, and deny the public access to information."

"We have even gotten to the point where editors write what I call 'advertorials' to appease companies—false editorials that invariably praise their corporate advertisers," Balile said.

There is similar editorial pressure from corporate advertisers in Uganda. "They seek more editorial visibility than government advertisers," said Robert Kabushenga, the chief executive officer of Uganda's leading state daily, *New Vision*. "Occasionally they demand spiking negative stories or suspend advertising to 'punish' for adverse publicity. The threat is that we are dependent on their money in an increasingly tight market."

Certain companies, banks, and cell-phone companies, for example, have become difficult for the Kenyan press to cover because of the revenue they provide, said Charles Onyango-Obbo, executive editor at the Nation Media Group. In July, Equity Bank's cash machines stopped working for several days but only online news publications and social media covered the story, according to local journalists. "I think the bank was effective in limiting bad publicity. They post a lot of ads and its boss is known to many media CEOs. They play golf together," *Daily Nation* reporter Aggrey Mutambo said.

Sometimes the news is also tainted because of desired support from nongovernmental organizations and the United Nations. This is especially noticeable in South Sudan, which relies heavily on the U.N. and NGOs in its rebuilding process. "It has been my experience that managing editors who have attained adverts from U.N. agencies and NGOs often assign reporters to positively cover their activities," South Sudanese freelance journalist Joseph Edward said. This appears to have less to do with outside organizations urging coverage of their activities, and more to do with providing positive coverage in hopes of financial support through advertisements and grants, Edward said.

Self-censorship also arises when politicians and businessmen own or invest in media outlets, an issue that especially troubles the Kenyan and South Sudanese press.

Generally praised by the media community for his editorial hands-off approach to the press, the princely rich Aga Khan, spiritual head of the 15-million-strong Ismaili community, owns 47 percent of the shares in the Nation Media Group. Three journalists at the *Daily Nation*, requesting anonymity to protect their jobs, say that, as a result, his investments in tourism and finance are almost never criticized in the East African press. This appears to be more a reflection of staff loyalty than any direct pressure, but is self-censorship nevertheless.

Meanwhile, Daniel Arap Moi, Kenya's former president, is believed to own the majority of shares in the Standard Media Group, according to a January report by the media development organization Internews and news reports. Moi's protégé, Uhuru Kenyatta, Kenya's recently elected president, owns the Mediamax Company that prints *The People* newspaper, along with K24 television and Kameme FM, the same report said.

"If you follow the Standard Media Group, you will not see negative coverage of former President Moi. If you follow Mediamax, the same applies to the current leadership," said George Nyabuga, a journalism lecturer at the University of Nairobi. Standard Media Group chief editor John Bundotich and Mediamax head of news Anderson Waweru both denied this assertion.

According to an independent study conducted by South Sudanese journalist Godfrey Victor Bulla, eight of 11 newspapers in circulation in South Sudan are either directly or indirectly government-owned.

■ ■ ■

Commercial pressures on reporters and editors are not confined to the recruiting and retention of advertisers. As in many Western newsrooms, there is an increasing focus on cost-cutting and profits—even ad spending is on the rise in places such as Kenya. According to the Newspaper Association of America, newspaper advertising revenue fell 6 percent in 2012 in the United States and is expected to decline further as newspapers increasingly rely on revenue from circulation. Not so in Kenya. In the first quarter of 2012, 18 billion Kenyan shillings (roughly US$212 million) was spent on advertising, according to the research company Ipsos Synovate, while 12 billion Kenyan shillings (roughly US$141 million) was spent in the same period in 2011.

In a presentation at a media forum in Naivasha, Kenya, in October 2013, Harun Mwangi, chief executive of the statutory regulator Media Council of Kenya, said newsrooms are increasingly focused on making money rather than reporting news. This is largely because most media owners are also big business players, Mwangi said: "They only focus on issues of public concern in the media as long as it bears profits."

In order to cut costs, investigative journalism has been curtailed and replaced by public relations exercises, with "news" fed to reporters, Mwangi said. Increasingly, media companies are encouraging their staff to attain degrees in business rather than journalism, he added, based on his experience working with Kenyan editors and journalists at the council.

Similar pressures on news managers occur in Uganda, with editors assigned commercial targets, according to the *Daily Monitor*'s Wanyama. On his personal blog, Wanyama wrote that editors are now expected to reach sales targets and initiate "money-making" projects, adding, "So, beyond being bogged down with the pressure of delivering good stories, editors must think about special projects that will yield extra revenue for the paper." In an interview with CPJ, he provided an example: "An editorial initiative such as a feature on health, for instance, will be cut for something that brings in money, so we are forced to cover areas where there is money even if there is not much public interest [in the topic]."

The tussle between moneymaking and news making has always been there, Uganda's Among said, but the tension is growing. "I fear we are abandoning our core business, the editorial business, and focusing on the profit margins. It's affecting the quality of journalism," she said.

While corporate influence in the newsroom is clearly a global phenomenon, editors and media analysts believe the problem is especially acute in East Africa. According to Mireny, of Tanzania's Media Council, in strong and mature market economies, where literacy rates are high, advertisers have less of a stranglehold over a newspaper's independence. In emerging economies, such as those in East Africa, with limited competition and often low literacy and circulation rates, editors are more vulnerable to outside pressures.

Small publishers in small economies are the most vulnerable. "Why this is particularly hard in Uganda," said James Tumusiime, the managing editor of the independent weekly *Observer*, "is because the economy is small, so advertisers are only a handful and you don't want to lose the major ones. It is even harder for smaller newspapers, because while some companies find they cannot do without the biggest daily, they can easily withdraw advertising from smaller ones."

Newspapers can never be fully independent in Rwanda, said Christopher Kayumba, a lecturer and media expert at the National University of Rwanda, because the newspapers rely on just a handful of advertisers, the government being one of the most influential.

■ ■ ■

Who are these advertisers in East Africa who hold such editorial influence over the press?

Across the region, the government still wields the most influence, despite increasing numbers of private companies buying ad space. Even then, Kenyan companies that advertise heavily are often financially linked to the government, said media consultant Gatchie.

The Kenyan government is the largest shareholder, for instance, at Kenya Commercial Bank, and the Kenyan subsidiaries of Standard Chartered and Barclays Bank. It is also one of the largest shareholders of Safaricom, the country's leading telecommunications company.

Then there is direct advertising by the government. According to the chairman of the Kenyan Commission for Administrative Justice, Otiende Amollo, the government spent roughly 26 million Kenyan shillings (US$297,500) in just two weeks on congratulatory messages in newspapers to politicians in presidential and legislative elections held in March 2013.

In Rwanda, approximately 85 to 90 percent of advertisements come from the public sector, says Robert Mugabe, editor of the online news site *Great Lakes Voice*. "If you need to attract adverts, it's simple. Don't annoy government," he said.

Government money constitutes roughly 60 percent of the advertising revenue of newspapers in Tanzania, Balile said. This crucial revenue is often provided to publications that support the government, Mireny said, disadvantaging independent publications.

The survival instincts of the dominant political elite in East Africa, where opposition parties maintain marginal influence, ensure government advertisers apply pressure on the press. In Kenya, as elsewhere, the ruling party maintains near monopolistic control over ads in the media, said William Oloo Janak, chairman of the Kenya Correspondent's Association.

Government advertising is so pervasive that some publications are launched purely to milk the flow of money. While Tanzania has roughly 16 active dailies, Balile said, there are 767 registered newspapers. "During local government elections, 450 publications suddenly appear on the newsstands. During a presidential election, you'll see all 767 papers vying for state adverts," he said.

Similarly, in Kenya, temporary and wholly government-supported publications have a short lifespan but make a lot of money while being printed, said *Daily Nation* online editor Charles Omondi in Nairobi. Under the authoritarian leadership of Moi, he said, all state advertising was channelled through the Moi government's daily mouthpiece, the *Kenya Times*, and state officials were expected to purchase a copy. But "with Moi out of power, *Kenya Times* became '*Kenya Sometimes*,' with irregular printing, before folding," he said.

Some East African governments often point to large numbers of publications as evidence that the media in their countries are free. In a public address in January 2013, Tanzanian President Jakaya Kikwete boasted that the country had registered 763 newspapers and publications, the largest number in Africa, according to news reports. But a plethora of newspapers does not equal press freedom, especially when the majority function as a government mouthpiece.

When the majority of media houses agreed to blanket advertising from the ruling party in Tanzania during the 2010 general elections, the Swahili daily, *Mwananchi*, or *Citizen*, did not, said Mireny, of Tanzania's Media Council. "The post-election sales proved that audiences are not fools," he said. "Time and again, papers that failed the impartiality test during campaigns and thereafter have seen their sales drifting downwards." Progovernment papers such as *Uhuru* and *Habari Leo*, for example, only manage to survive through government advertising and never through sales, *Raia Mwema* News Director Islam said.

The former highly critical weekly, *MwanaHalisi*, was starved of government ad revenue due to its critical stance, Managing Editor Saed Kubenea said. But the paper's brave and unique voice attracted a large readership, its circulation at one point reaching 100,000, the highest in Tanzania, local journalists said. It may well be the sole example in the region of a newspaper's survival due largely to its circulation. "I think we were one of the few in East Africa who managed to thrive through sales alone," Kubenea said. Its critical success irked the government so much that the newspaper was accused of sedition and banned indefinitely in July 2012.

■ ■ ■

Eventually, online news outlets and social media may provide an alternative to newspapers. In Kenya, in particular, the popularity of social media as an outlet for breaking and critical news was evident during the September 2013 terrorist siege of Westgate Mall in Nairobi.

"Recent events in Kenya have me increasingly believe that online platforms as leveraged by ordinary citizens are growing more critical of state affairs than the mainstream press," said Nanjira Sambuli, a mathematician and new media strategist.

Still, Internet growth is slow and it is not clear how online news outlets will earn revenue. The International Telecommunications Union indicates that Internet usage in East Africa—with the exception of South Sudan, for which statistics are not yet available—increased in total by 10 percent over the past five years.

Newspapers, then, will continue to dominate the region for some time. The hope lies in media owners across East Africa accepting that the longevity of their newspapers does not depend as much on profits from advertising as it does on professional editorial policies that will secure the loyalty of readers.

**Tom Rhodes** *is CPJ's East Africa representative, based in Nairobi. Rhodes is a founder of South Sudan's first independent newspaper.*

# 5

# CONTROLLING THE NARRATIVE

# Would-Be Repressors Brandish "Ethics" as Justification

*By Jean-Paul Marthoz*

The *News of the World* scandal, in which the British Sunday tabloid hacked voicemails of celebrities and ordinary citizens, led to a divisive debate on how to regulate the media in the UK.

*Source:* Reuters/Luke MacGregor.

A ll around the planet, authoritarian rulers and their officials hold forth about the "responsibility of the press."

Most of the time, their preaching and talk of the need for codes of conduct or ethical guidelines serve to clip the wings of independent journalists and tame the press. Their invocation of lofty notions of patriotism, honor, reputation, and respect for authority are meant to deter investigations and exposés of their abuses of power or ill-acquired wealth.

Ethics are also brandished when the press covers sensitive subjects, such as religion, nationalism, or ethnicity. Under the pretext of protecting minorities against hate speech, or of preventing incitement to violence, governments often strive to censor stories that are in the public interest and should be told.

In authoritarian countries, calls for journalists to exercise a sense of responsibility or decency are mostly code for censorship. In Egypt, after the overthrow of the Muslim Brotherhood–led government in July 2013, the new military-backed rulers immediately announced their intention to create a journalistic code of ethics and made its adoption a condition for lifting existing censorship.

In Ecuador, President Rafael Correa has been indulging in media bashing for years, calling journalists "unethical," "trash-talking," or "liars." After his landslide re-election in February 2013, he warned, as reported by CPJ correspondent John Otis, that "one thing that has to be fixed is the press, which totally lacks ethics and scruples." Correa has since "fixed" the press through a new communications law that severely restricts press freedom by establishing government regulation of editorial content and giving the authorities power to impose arbitrary sanctions on the press.

In June 2013, the Sri Lankan government tried to impose a new code of media ethics in order, according to Keheliya Rambukwella, the minister of mass media and information, "to create a salutary media culture." Although the protests of national and international journalists associations forced the government to backtrack, some observers fear that the code might resurface. "The media code was part of a sustained campaign to control the media and curtail dissent," Brad Adams, the Asia director for Human Rights Watch, told CPJ. "Its vagueness would likely have led to greater self-censorship to avoid government retaliation." The code prohibited "criticisms affecting foreign relations" and content "that promotes anti-national attitudes." It also forbade "material against the integrity of the Executive, Judiciary and Legislature" and warned against the publication of content that "offends against expectations of the public morality of the country or tend to lower the standards of public taste and morality."

In Burundi, "The discussions around the drafting of the new Press Law, which was promulgated in June 2013, constantly referred to the alleged ethical breaches of the press," Marie-Soleil Frère, a Brussels University researcher and author, told CPJ. "Members of the ruling party repeated ad nauseam that journalists are biased, unfair, and indulge in defamation, lies and insults."

Authoritarian governments also have a way of playing up alleged ethical breaches when it fits their interests in order to discredit troublesome journalists and even to downplay physical assaults on reporters at work.

If a Mexican or Honduran journalist on the drug beat is murdered, some police use the expression *"Por algo sera,"* which means, "There must have been a reason"—implying the death was justified by the reporter's involvement with criminal organizations. That is used as a justification for not seriously investigating the murder and feeds the cycle of impunity.

In fact, the governments that have been the most vocal in calling for "ethical journalism" have often been the first to push their news media to break all journalistic rules and standards. In Egypt, where the new military-civilian authorities have been calling for ethics in journalism, state-owned media have been engaged in ruthless campaigns against dissenting journalistic voices.

"Astonishingly, Egyptian journalists have also participated in the harassment of officially unpopular colleagues," said Mohamed Khattab, a journalist with the *Freedom and Justice* newspaper, the official voice of the Muslim Brotherhood, on a July 12, 2013, NPR broadcast. These attacks have not spared international media. "At an army press conference this week," added BBC reporter Andrew Hosken during the same broadcast, "an Al-Jazeera reporter was ejected by his peers while they chanted 'Out, out,' and then applauded when he'd gone."

In Azerbaijan, pro-government media have shamelessly invaded the privacy of leading opponents and independent journalists and published rumors and lies without consequence. "I have seen count-less examples of deliberately unprofessional and unethical behavior from state and pro-government media," Rebecca Vincent, the advocacy director of the Baku-based Human Rights Club, told CPJ. In August 2013, for instance, *Ses* newspaper, which is affiliated with the ruling party, published an article attacking Khadija Ismayilova, an award-winning critical journalist working with Radio Free Europe/ Radio Liberty (RFE/RL). The title was "Khadija's Armenian Mother Should Die." In a press release, RFE/RL said: "The article falsely labeled sev-eral of Ismayilova's relatives Armenian. For some Azeris, the reference to 'Armenian' ethnicity is code for treason in a country that went to war with Armenia over disputed territory in 1988."

State media in Ecuador are used as a powerful megaphone to smear journalists who do not toe the official line. Likewise, "in Burundi, Rema FM, a pro-governmental radio [station], spends its time slam-ming radio stations close to civil society," Frère said.

In such countries, governments connive with some of the media to violate the most basic ethical norms. The placement of advertising by the state, for instance, is regularly used as a murky tool to secure slavish or toothless coverage. The tactic directly undermines the image of a free press as financially independent and able to avoid conflicts of interest.

In Argentina, this arbitrary pressure is applied at the national level, but its impact is particularly strong on smaller, provincial media outlets, "many of whom," CPJ's Sara Rafsky wrote in 2012, "are almost com-pletely financially dependent on official advertising and therefore vul-nerable to government pressure over their coverage."

"Brown envelopes" handed to individual journalists serve the same purpose and have the same effect: They gravely undermine the inde-pendence and the freedom of the press. In some countries, where selective ad placements and direct payments to reporters are com-mon, this routine is even defended by some inside the profession with the argument that official ads and personal tips are essential to protect media incomes and journalists' jobs.

Media owners in some countries are also constrained by their business links with the state and therefore are susceptible to the latter's capacity to cajole or punish. In the worst such cases, the vulnerability to state pressure occurs when a media company owns other businesses whose prosperity depends on public works tenders or government licenses.

In Turkey, during the protests in Taksim Square and Gezi Park in May and June of 2013, major privately owned news organizations acted as proxy state censors in several ways, including abstaining from covering the events, stigmatizing the protesters, and adopting the government's line. To the continuing amusement of many, CNN Türk TV aired a documentary on penguins rather than provide coverage of the demonstrations, turning penguins into a national symbol of self-censorship.

"They have acted proactively, not waiting for memos from the state to censor their journalists," said Aidan White, founder of the Ethical Journalism Initiative and former general secretary of the International Federation of Journalists.

"The country's journalists are enslaved in newsrooms run by greedy and ruthless media proprietors, whose economic interests make them submissive to" Prime Minister Recep Tayyip Erdoğan, wrote Yavuz Baydar, a leading Turkish columnist who was fired in July 2013 from his post as ombudsman of the daily *Sabah* after writing articles critical of the government's handling of the Taksim Square/Gezi Park movements. "Direct criticism of government policies on the Kurds, Syria, or corruption, has led to many columnists being fired or 'boycotted.' The scope of democratic debate and dissemination of opinion has narrowed severely," he wrote.

The stakes are high. The history of attacks against the press tells us that journalists like *El Espectador* director Guillermo Cano in Colombia, *Novaya Gazeta's* Anna Politkovskaya in Russia and *Agos* editor Hrant Dink in Turkey were killed because the ethical vision of their work led them to confront thuggish groups or corrupt power elites. "Journalists who are committed to their work are killed precisely because they refuse to be corrupted and to submit to criminal gangs," a leading Mexican editor, who asked not to be named because of the security risks, told CPJ.

Yet, unethical journalism can also trigger attacks against the press by inviting crippling defamation suits or even violence as radical political groups or criminal organizations retaliate against journalists who publish unsubstantiated accusations or take sides. "I firmly believe that the best security measure a journalist can take is to be honest, objective, ethically responsible, and really independent," a Latin American journalist told the authors of "Killing the Messenger," a 2007 report by the International News Safety Institute.

Unethical journalists also weaken solidarity and therefore contribute to the cycle of violence and impunity. "As some murdered journalists are associates of criminal organizations, the gangs and even the police may more easily dismiss our denunciations and blur their own responsibility in these attacks against the press," the Mexican editor told CPJ. "And the profession appears uncomfortable and divided on how to respond."

Likewise, ethical breaches undermine public support for the media and provide an opportunity, even in established democracies, for governments to adopt tougher statutory regulations. In countries like Venezuela and Russia, when the media came under state pressure the public was not moved, as if all journalists were identified with their unethical colleagues.

The *News of the World* scandal—the hacking of the voicemails of celebrities and ordinary citizens by the British Sunday tabloid—is one of the most glaring examples of the negative impact of ruffian journalism on freedom of the press in a democracy.

The scandal has rocked the U.K. media scene ever since it was exposed in 2010. It led to a public inquiry and to such a popular outcry that politicians felt obliged to act—or at least to appear to act—against press barons whom many of them, until then, had greatly feared and assiduously courted. By doing so, they took the risk of adopting ill-considered and hasty regulations that might chill press freedom under the cover of punishing a crime.

The link between journalists' real or alleged failings and state overreaction is evident. "In South Africa, the ANC introduced in 2010—but failed to enforce—a project aimed at setting up a Media Appeals Tribunal that would curtail the power of the [self-regulatory] Press Council, arguing that the ombudsmen system was expensive and ineffectual to correct the journalists' shortcomings," Frère, the Brussels University researcher, told CPJ.

South Africa is not the only country where journalists have adopted press codes or set up press councils in order to ward off government regulation. The Press Complaints Commission in Britain was set up in 1991 by a committee of editors to avoid the creation of a statutory council, according to the U.K.-based free expression group Article 19. Likewise, the creation of a Conseil de déontologie journalistique, or journalist ethics council, in Belgium in 2009 came on the heels of pressure from political parties to act after some Belgian media were accused of crossing red lines in covering a series of child abductions and pedophilia cases.

The tension between press freedom and ethics means "balancing rights and duties," Belgian academic and author Benoît Grevisse told CPJ. This exercise largely depends on the doctrine of journalism to which one adheres. The school of public interest journalism has made its attachment to ethics an essential element of the exercise of press freedom. All quality media consider the respect of high standards as a lever and not as an impediment to press freedom. "A democratic society needs a genuinely free, independent, and responsible, press to dig deep and then dig even deeper," Carl Bernstein of Watergate fame wrote in *Newsweek* in 2011 in an essay on the *News of the World* hacking scandal.

Some authors go further. Stephen A. Ward, director of the Center for Journalism Ethics at the University of Wisconsin, argued in his 2011 book, *Ethics and the Media*, that the role of a free press and journalism "goes beyond simply exercising its freedom to publish to an ethical concern for how it facilitates public discourse in a pluralistic society." White of the Ethical Journalism Initiative told CPJ, "Journalism has a public purpose which is to provide, as honestly and as independently as possible, accurate and reliable intelligence for the communities it serves."

This civic-oriented journalism, however, is just one of many legitimate forms that reflect different criteria and missions, such as commercially-driven or "libertarian" journalism. And, like it or not, bad journalism is also journalism. Unethical methods—not to be confused with criminal acts like phone hacking—are inevitably part of a vibrant and rowdy press scene. Many worry that attempts to eliminate them completely through regulation and sanctions would entail undue risks for everyone in the media.

In his book *La Civilización del Espectáculo* (the civilization of entertainment), published in 2012, Mario Vargas Llosa, winner of the Nobel Prize in Literature, recognized that "scandal-driven journalism is the perverse stepson of the culture of freedom. You cannot suppress it without dealing a deadly blow to freedom of expression."

One of the strongest advocates of socially responsible journalism, the Hutchins Commission on Freedom of the Press, concurs. In its landmark report, "A Free and Responsible Press," published in 1947, it said: "The attempt to correct abuses of freedom, including press freedom, by resort to legal penalties and controls is the first spontaneous impulse of reform. But the dangers of the cure must be weighed against the dangers of the disease; every definition of an abuse invites abuse of the definition. Hence many a lying, venal, and scoundrelly public expression must continue to find shelter under a 'freedom of the press' built for widely different ends. There is a practical presumption against the use of legal action to curb press abuse."

Self-regulation has become a mantra within many journalists associations. They see it as a key instrument to uphold freedom of expression while deterring state interference. However, even though many democratic countries, especially in Western Europe, have established press councils and adopted codes of ethics that are not seen as chilling the press, the suspicion remains that these media accountability systems might chip away at the audacity that true press freedom allows. For skeptics, the call to be responsible, to limit harm, risks being interpreted in ways that could—ostensibly for the good of the country and the peace of the community—deter journalists and editors from working on sensitive stories related to national security, racial relations, or religious tensions.

"Suppose that in 1971 some code of ethics, official or otherwise, had persuaded Arthur Sulzberger not to publish the top-secret Pentagon Papers. It is doubtful that any code would have urged him to publish the government's supposed secrets," Tom Wicker, former associate editor of *The New York Times*, wrote in his book, *On the Record: An Insider's Guide to Journalism*. "There is no substitute for a journalist's integrity, sense of honor, and desire to be responsible. A specific code of ethics is a poor replacement for any of those attributes. Codes enjoin caution, limit choices, and invoke the conventional wisdom. They do not usually encourage bravery, risk-taking and challenging the status quo."

To some, journalism is a profession of freebooters. In his 2007 book, *Freedom for the Thought We Hate: A Biography of the First Amendment*, Anthony Lewis quoted the *London Times* columnist Bernard Levin as saying: "The press has no duty to be responsible at all, and it will be an ill day for freedom if it should ever acquire one. We are and must remain vagabonds and outlaws, for only by so remaining shall we be able to keep the faith by which we live, which is the pursuit of knowledge that others would like unpursued and the making of comments that others would prefer unmade."

Still, even if the virtue police might be more dangerous for a free society than reporters on the loose, the partisans of press freedom cannot wipe their hands and move on. In many cases, as we have seen in some of the examples above, a pervasive culture of ethical failings genuinely compromises journalism and threatens media independence. "Despots love to see a free press behaving badly," wrote former *New York Times* Executive Editor Bill Keller in the wake of the *News of the World* scandal. "Even more, they love to see a free government reacting badly."

There is no way to shirk the discussion. "We have been so much engaged in defending journalists, that we become shy sometimes in uncovering or exposing the dark side of our craft," Rosental Alves, director of the Knight Center for Journalism in the Americas at the University of Texas, said in an interview with Bill Ristow published by the Center for International Media Assistance in 2010.

Press freedom groups should energetically take back the ethical flag from the hands of those—despots and other pseudo-moralists—who hijack it. "Ethics should be upheld in order to avoid the dangerous tendency of state authorities to ask for more control," Aidan White said.

"Ethics does not only entail duties and prohibitions," Grevisse, the Belgian author, told CPJ. "It also includes rights so that journalists can assume their particular responsibilities towards the public." Press freedom in fact is often a precondition to practicing ethical journalism. "The ability to report ethically has an essential characteristic: journalistic independence," Peter Horrocks, BBC director for global news, said at an African conference in August 2013.

Fighting for high ethical standards in the name of press freedom is a good way to irritate the Robert Mugabes, the Rafael Correas, and the Abdel Fattah el-Sisis of the world and deprive them of an easy alibi to discredit and silence critical journalism.

*CPJ Senior Adviser **Jean-Paul Marthoz** is a Belgian journalist and writer. He is a foreign affairs columnist for* Le Soir *and journalism professor at the Université catholique de Louvain.*

# Pressure on Journalists Rises Along With Africa's Prospects

## By Mohamed Keita

A newspaper displayed in the Ikoyi district of Lagos on September 30, 2013, tells of a deadly attack on a college in northeast Nigeria by suspected Boko Haram militants. Coverage of the group can be sensitive in Nigeria.

*Source:* Reuters/Akintunde Akinleye.

When terrorists stormed Nairobi's upmarket Westgate mall, they not only damaged Kenya's image as a safe tourist and business destination but also spoiled the popular narrative of an emerging, hopeful continent.

Out of the tragedy came a call for unity behind leaders and security forces, but as awkward questions about government missteps emerged, Interior Minister Joseph Lenku accused the press of not being patriotic enough. Later on, Police Inspector-General David Kimaiyo threatened to arrest investigative journalists John Allan Namu and Mohammed Ali of KTN Television over a broadcast that raised embarrassing questions about the conduct and coordination of security forces at the time of the attack. "You cannot provoke propaganda and incite Kenyans against the authorities," Kimaiyo told a press conference, according to news reports. "We must be loyal to the system and the government of the day," added Criminal Investigation Department Director Ndegwa Muhoro.

Pressuring journalists to shape news coverage in the name of patriotism and unity is not new, least of all in Africa. Yet, after a decade of unprecedented economic growth and infrastructure development on the continent, the stakes are higher than ever. Persistent challenges and inconvenient truths—such as the resilience of the Somali terrorist group which claimed responsibility for Westgate, and the Kenyan authorities' lack of preparation for such an attack—could dent optimism, give pause to donors and investors, and threaten the standing of those in power. Politicians and other authorities feel a strong incentive to suppress reports of such problems.

"I think the dominant story—about growth, or innovation, or whatever is pleasing at the moment in the corridors of power—comes at the expense of the countless other stories that need to be told," author Siddhartha Deb told CPJ.

Two years after CPJ explored how media restrictions are justified by invoking the primacy of economic development over democracy and human rights, the insistence on positive news remains a significant threat to press freedom in Africa.

■ ■ ■

The African Union marked its 50th anniversary in 2013 extolling an "African Renaissance" and celebrating a sense of optimism. The new Africa is "a rising continent, a confident continent, which understands its challenges but also is aware of the opportunities it has," said Antonio M.A. Pedro, director of the East Africa office of the United Nations Economic Commission for Africa. Pedro told CPJ that rich human and natural resources, some of the fastest growing economies in the world, business opportunities, and an improved risk profile make Africa an increasingly attractive area for investment.

Yet, as *Guardian* correspondent David Smith wrote in October, the popular narrative of "Africa rising" does not take into account that the continent's economic growth is not trickling down to the daily lives of the majority of Africans. Smith referred to an October report by the independent research group Afrobarometer that suggested that a decade of economic boom had failed to substantially improve poverty levels in most African countries.

Furthermore, the sustainability of Africa's growth is far from certain. The World Bank's December 2012 assessment highlighted its vulnerability to any slump in China, the continent's number-one trade partner. A March report by the UN Development Program found that despite registering some of the world's most dramatic improvements in life expectancy, education, and standard of living between 2000 and 2011, sub-Saharan Africa still accounts for the world's lowest levels of human development. In a 2012 report, the Africa Progress Panel found that widening inequality, endemic corruption, and bad governance crippled the pace of development and maintained the continent's dependence on aid.

"My perspective is that Africa is still struggling to prosper," said Thomas Bwire, news editor of Pamoja FM, a community radio station based in Nairobi's Kibera slum, the largest shantytown in Africa.

Yet some journalists say the motivation to play up Africa's positive image is based on a noble impulse to counter international news coverage long dominated by wars, coups, famine, ruthless villains, miserable people, and happy animals. "For centuries, the continent has not been able to tell the history of its nations and people through an African perspective," said Amadou Mahtar Ba, chief executive of the African Media Initiative, a pan-African media development group.

That tension played out publicly ahead of the March 2013 presidential election in Kenya, after CNN reported what many viewers felt was an unbalanced and exaggerated look at the threat of ethnic violence. Angry Twitter users created a hashtag, #someonetellCNN, and aired their grievances about errant or sensationalist global media coverage. (CNN stood by its coverage.) In May, freshly elected President Uhuru Kenyatta criticized international reporting on his country and exhorted local journalists to counter it. "These are the images that we must aggressively seek to banish from the global media space and sphere about Africa," he said. "Africa is rising and we must communicate this to our people and the world. We rely on you, the media, to correct these [negative] images and propagate the new positive developments in our continent."

■ ■ ■

In Nigeria, officials castigate the press for failing to report what the government sees as success stories. In January 2013, at a gathering of professionals in marketing, public relations, advertising, and the media, Sen. Ike Nwachukwu, a former military general and minister of foreign affairs, declared that the Nigerian press should stop embarrassing the nation and instead protect its image, according to news reports. "I am not asking for cover-ups, but publications that impact negatively or ridicule our country and its citizenry should not be made," Nwachukwu said. This criticism came as the government earmarked US$4.2 million for public relations to promote a message of transformation and development, according to the federal budget.

Tolu Ogunlesi, a freelancer who contributes to the Nigerian business magazine *Ventures Africa*, rejected the notion that the local press neglects positive developments. "There are a good number of positive stories—of entrepreneurship, of people struggling against all odds to do inspiring things. The truth is that there's a lot of depressing stuff that happens, so if that seems to dominate the news, then it's clearly just a case of journalism imitating reality," he said.

Nigerian authorities use an assortment of direct and indirect legal, financial, and brutal means to suppress scrutinizing press reports on certain topics. Of particular sensitivity in Nigeria are stories about the terrorist group Boko Haram and security policies to combat this threat. In 2013, security forces detained and intimidated journalists of the weekly *Al-Mizan* over an investigative report on alleged extrajudicial detentions of terrorism suspects.

Reporting on political and corruption scandals also draws official ire. Editors from *Leadership* newspaper were harassed and sued for forgery in 2013 after publishing what they maintain was a memo by President Goodluck Jonathan that described plans to increase gas prices and to sabotage a merger of opposition parties ahead of the 2015 general elections. The journalists could face up to life in prison, according to CPJ's review of the Nigerian penal code. The government also banned a documentary film on corruption in the state's management of oil wealth.

In Ethiopia, the leadership is often credited with fast economic growth, strides in health and education, and bold policies to modernize infrastructure and agriculture and boost hydropower. Yet this misses a wider context, some Ethiopian journalists say. "I cannot deny that there are some improvements in some aspects, but all these are good [only] when we compare them with the former regimes," Muluken Tesfaw, a reporter with the weekly *Ethio-Mihdar*, told CPJ. "We cannot compete with our neighbors in many cases." Muluken pointed to the state's absolute monopoly of the telecom sector as an example. Ethiopia ranked in the bottom third of the African Development Bank's Africa Competitiveness Report and scored below the sub-Saharan average in business innovation, financial market development, and technological readiness.

Ordinary Ethiopians face a rising cost of living, joblessness, and a stranglehold on the economy by the ruling party, the Ethiopian People's Revolutionary Democratic Front (EPRDF). Membership in the party determines access to opportunities, which has led to a sense of hopelessness among the youth, rising prostitution, emigration, and more beggars in the streets, Muluken said. An award-winning journalist who wrote extensive critiques of these policies, Reeyot Alemu, has been imprisoned since 2011 on trumped-up terrorism charges and is serving a five-year sentence. Her Amharic-language newspaper *Feteh* was banned a few weeks after her arrest.

A March 2013 report by the EPRDF said the media "should work on the burning questions of the public at large in a positive, problem solving, and participatory way . . . for we are aware of the negative impacts of the international neoliberal media and communication industry." The international perception of Ethiopia has been distorted by the government's tight control of information, including the banning of independent newspapers and the imprisonment of prominent journalists.

Among the untold stories are that of small-scale farmers evicted from their land to make way for commercial agribusiness companies. In May, Muluken was detained in northwest Ethiopia for 10 days after he gathered from displaced farmers their allegations of official coercion, abuse, and violence. In November, in the western region of Gambella, local authorities briefly detained international photojournalist Robin Hammond when he attempted to interview farmers on their views of commercial farming in the area, according to news reports and local journalists. The government has consistently denied allegations of abuse and coercion, but the accusations are persistent enough that the World Bank in July ordered its independent Inspection Panel to conduct a full investigation.

■ ■ ■

Even in South Africa, which is widely seen as having one of the most free presses on the continent, officials castigate the independent press for being too negative. "Every morning you feel like you must leave this country because the reporting concentrates on the opposite of the positive," President Jacob Zuma told journalism students in September 2013 in Cape Town. Zuma called for "patriotic reporting," as practiced in Mexico, where, he said, journalists did not report on crime because it would tarnish the national image and scare off investors. (In fact, CPJ research shows that journalists in Mexico avoid reporting on crime out of fear for their lives. At least 20 journalists have been killed directly for their work in Mexico in the past decade, and dozens more murdered in unclear circumstances.)

Following an outcry over his remarks, Zuma's office issued a statement that mainly repeated his claim that negative coverage was fed by commercial pressures. "It is the expectation of the Presidency that these matters are discussed in newsrooms daily to ensure that the business side of the media does not negatively impact on the telling of the South African story," the statement read. In a meeting with CPJ, presidential spokesman Mac Maharaj backed away from defining "the South African story," but criticized what he called "negative-minded" reports.

Sean Jacobs, a South African-born author, professor at the New School University in New York, and the founder of the influential blog *Africa Is a Country*, rejects this notion. "People need to stop taking this 'potential investors' mumbo jumbo seriously. Governments are accountable to citizens, not investors," he said. "The idea that 'potential investors' will be scared off by accountability journalism exposing corrupt practices is ludicrous," he added. "Some of the world's most notoriously corrupt countries are also the most attractive to investors—not that their investment is of much good to ordinary people."

Under acting chief operations officer Hlaudi Motsoeneng, the South African Broadcasting Corporation (SABC), the government-run public broadcaster, has repeatedly censored content deemed offensive to Zuma and the ruling African National Congress, according to CPJ research. In an August interview with the weekly *Mail & Guardian*, Motsoeneng said, "I believe, from the SABC's side, 70 percent should be positive [news] stories and then you can have 30 percent negative stories."

For Mzilikazi wa Afrika, chair of the Forum of African Investigative Reporters, the notion that media do not report enough "good" news is baseless. "If you read newspapers in South Africa, there would be a story about government ministers donating houses or opening roads and clinics, even when those houses collapse and those clinics become white elephants or are understaffed—we report about that too."

Motsoeneng is not alone in wanting to prescribe a formula for news coverage. In September, Yolande Makolo, spokesman for Rwandan President Paul Kagame, criticized Western media in response to a *New York Times* interview of Kagame that highlighted sharply divided opinions about him. "I am sorry but 'balance' hurts Rwandans, and Africans. Even when stories reflect more positives than negatives, the positives don't carry as much weight overall as the negatives, which chip away at the agency we are working to accumulate. Balance thus erodes our reputation and standing in the global pecking order," she wrote in a letter published by *AllAfrica*.

Rwanda's disciplined leadership has delivered economic success, minimal corruption, clean roads, and safety, but years of suppression of the independent press has allowed the government to impose an unchallenged narrative of success, and Rwanda is frequently cited as a model of ethnic reconciliation. But while the government touts an egalitarian, inclusive society, the reality is much more complicated. For example, ethnic labels are officially banned from public discourse, yet the government refers to the 1994 genocide with an (exclusive) ethnic reference: "the 1994 Genocide against the Tutsi." Rwandan journalists risk arrest and criminal prosecution under harsh, overbroad laws against divisionism and genocide denial for contextualizing the country's achievements with such paradoxes, or giving voice to the social injustices that persist.

■ ■ ■

"More often than not, the news from or about the continent that the rest of the world sees is obsessed with extreme scenarios—the outlying evils and the outlying good. We don't get enough nuance, enough non-sensational reporting about Africa," said Ogunlesi, the Nigerian freelancer with *Ventures Africa*.

Indeed, throughout Africa, journalists need the assurance that reporting facts, even if they challenge those in power or popular national programs, is not seen as disloyalty—or worse, such as illegal or dangerous to their well-being. Navigating the fine lines that separate journalism from public relations is not easy, but in free societies, such determinations must always be left to journalists.

Charles Onyango-Obbo, executive editor of the Nation Media Group in Nairobi, says every story and every perspective is important. "Yes, there is a need to tell the African story, but I reject the idea that it can only be told by Africans. The African story is a global story, and it is open to everyone who tells it, from their point of view."

As Sudanese billionaire Mo Ibrahim put it in an October column in *Mail & Guardian*, "We have to guard against the 'Africa Rising' or 'the hopeful continent' headlines—just as in the past when it was wrong to dismiss Africa as a 'basket case' or a 'hopeless continent.'" He added, "We need to move decisively away from both Afro-optimistic and Afro-pessimistic headlines towards 'Afro-realism.'"

**Mohamed Keita** *is advocacy coordinator for CPJ's Africa Program. He has written about independent journalism and development in sub-Saharan Africa for publications including* The New York Times *and* Africa Review, *and has appeared on NPR, the BBC, Al-Jazeera, and Radio France Internationale.*

# Vietnam Tightens the Squeeze on Its Bloggers

## By Shawn W. Crispin

**Blogger Pham Viet Dao attends a conference on social media in Hanoi on December 24, 2012. Dao was arrested on June 13, 2013, on accusations of antistate activity.**

*Source:* Reuters/Nguyen Lan Thang.

When Vietnamese blogger Nguyen Lan Thang left his home in Hanoi to report on the trial of a group of political activists charged with anti-state crimes, he switched off his mobile phone to avoid government surveillance of his movements. Despite taking that precaution, the police raided the hotel where he was staying in the northern city of Vinh a day before the court hearing. Thang videotaped the raid from his balcony and posted the footage on his personal blog just minutes before he was arrested.

The police justified his detention without charge on the grounds that he had traveled to Vinh at a "sensitive" time. He and two other bloggers he traveled with were held in police custody for three days and were released only after the verdict in the two-day trial was announced on January 9, 2013. Thang says he was beaten during interrogations and later strip-searched by police officials looking for hidden digital camera memory cards.

"I'm a focal point for police," Thang told CPJ, adding that he has been detained and interrogated on "dozens" of occasions because of his blogging. "When there is a trial of activists or planned protests, they send plainclothes police to guard my house to make sure I don't leave." To dodge trailing officials, Thang said, he now leaves his house several days in advance of big news events and communicates only over foreign-hosted online platforms like Skype to avoid GPS tracking of his location.

Thang's experience is disturbingly typical of Vietnam's growing number of persecuted independent bloggers. With at least 14 journalists behind bars, Vietnam was Asia's second-worst jailer of the press, trailing only China, according to CPJ's 2012 prison survey. More bloggers have been arrested since. The majority of those held have been charged or convicted under draconian and vague anti-state laws for their blogging or online journalism, including postings critical of the Communist Party–dominated government, its leadership, or its policies. Among them is Nguyen Van Hai, known in Vietnam's blogosphere as Dieu Cay. A blogger who has been imprisoned since 2008, Hai is a recipient of CPJ's 2013 International Press Freedom Award.

Vietnam's government maintains some of the most severe media controls in Asia. All news media in the country are owned and controlled by the one-party state. There are no privately run news outlets.

A mushrooming blogosphere, however, has challenged the Communist Party's media monopoly in recent years, with a growing cadre of pseudonymous bloggers reporting stories and publishing commentaries that would be routinely censored in the mainstream press.

Forbidden topics include the activities of political dissidents and activists, factional divisions inside the Communist Party, human rights and pro-democracy issues, and any mention of ethnic differences between the country's once-divided northern and southern regions. Reporting on anti-China sentiment or protests related to territorial disputes or extractive industry investments is also barred. As the local economy shifts from strength to weakness, the authorities have also blocked criticism of the government's economic management, land conflicts between the government and local communities, and business dealings of top Communist Party members.

Beginning in 2008, the authorities have steadily clamped down on independent bloggers in a heavy-handed bid to bring the Internet under the same strict regulations and controls used to censor and guide the mainstream media's news coverage. The number of politically oriented bloggers has grown alongside fast-rising Internet penetration rates, estimated by government figures at 39.5 percent of the population in late 2012. In response to that perceived threat, the government intensified its campaign of repression in 2013 through harsh prison sentences, arrests, and new freedom-curbing legislation for governing the Internet.

In January 2013, five bloggers who contributed regularly to the Catholic Church-run *Vietnam Redemptorist News* were sentenced to harsh jail terms and follow-up periods of house arrest for various anti-state crimes, including "undermining national unity" and "propagandizing against the Socialist Republic of Vietnam."

In mid-year, three prominent bloggers—Dinh Nhat Uy, Pham Viet Dao, and Truong Duy Nhat—were detained on accusations that their blogging had "abused democratic freedoms," a charge outlined in Article 258 of the penal code that carries a sentence of up to seven years in prison. After a one-day trial, Uy was sentenced in October to a 15-month suspended prison sentence and one year of house arrest. The other two bloggers were still held without formal charge in late 2013.

Other bloggers critical of the government have endured severe abuse and humiliation. Blogger Nguyen Hoang Vi wrote a disturbing first-person account, posted on the *Danlambao* collective blog in January, about how police officials beat and stripped her and ordered state nurses to conduct a vaginal cavity search while she was in custody at Ho Chi Minh City's Nguyen Cu Trinh Ward. Officials said at the time that they suspected she had hidden "illegal exhibits" on her body and they videotaped the assault. In May, Vi and two family members were assaulted by state agents when she demanded officials return her confiscated cellphone and iPad in front of a Ho Chi Minh City police station, according to a Human Rights Watch report.

In another case of abuse, blogger Le Anh Hung, known for his opinionated postings on high-level corruption and abuse of power inside the Communist Party, was arrested on January 24, 2013, and committed against his will to a psychiatric institution. Before his arrest, Hung had been subjected to repeated interrogations, threats, and harassment by the police for his critical online writings. He was released 12 days after his arrest and soon resumed blogging, according to international news reports.

"Bloggers in Vietnam are living in fear," said Pham Doan Trang, speaking in Bangkok. A former newspaper reporter, she was fired in January 2013 for blogging independently on banned topics and leaking censored information to fellow bloggers. "All of us have reported on things that could be considered anti-state. We can be arrested at any time; it is always looming over us."

Those fears were compounded by a new decree enacted on September 1, 2013, that specifically targets bloggers and social media users. Among other restrictive provisions, Decree 72 on the Management, Provision, and Use of Internet Services and Online Information broadly prohibits Vietnamese bloggers and Internet users from linking to or reposting news from press organizations or information from foreign government websites.

The legislation was not explicit about how global Internet companies would be penalized for refusing to cooperate with official orders to identify or censor bloggers who use their online platforms to criticize the government, or for failing to filter keywords deemed sensitive, such as "democracy" or "human rights," from their local search engine results.

The decree also aims to place global Internet companies more firmly under Vietnamese law, although their servers are outside the country, with vaguely defined bans on any online postings hosted on their platforms that "go against the state of the Socialist Republic of Vietnam, jeopardize national security or social order, damage national unity, issue war propaganda, carry out acts of terrorism, create hatred between ethnic groups, or reveal state secrets, including those related to the military, security, and foreign affairs."

The Asia Internet Coalition, a group of multinational Internet companies including eBay, Facebook, and Google, said in a statement in response to the decree's announcement: "We believe that the Decree will negatively affect Vietnam's Internet ecosystem. In the long term, the Decree will stifle innovation and discourage businesses from operating in Vietnam, thereby hindering Vietnam's goal to establish itself as an advanced competitive ICT [information and communications technology] nation." Western governments, including the United States, also criticized the decree's restrictive provisions.

The criticism appeared initially to put officials on the defensive, underscoring the government's sensitivity to a potential reversal of foreign investment flows at a time of increasing economic weakness. Nguyen Thanh Huyen, head of the Ministry of Information's Online Information Section, told Reuters that Decree 72 had been "totally misunderstood." Said Huyen: "We never ban people from sharing information or linking news from websites. This is a normal decree which doesn't go against any human right commitments."

At a September 19 news conference in Denmark, which is one of Vietnam's largest foreign donors, President Truong Tan Sang told reporters his government was in the process of developing "a better platform for the political life of the people." In response to questions about the crackdown on bloggers, Sang acknowledged "defects" in Vietnam's politics, but insisted that "everybody . . . is equal before the law" and that there were "four million free bloggers in Vietnam."

Local bloggers believe the authorities are making preparations to eventually block Facebook and Google and replace them with local alternatives—similar to China's efforts to assert control over its Internet by developing indigenous search engines and social media services. A Russian-Vietnamese joint venture was reported by The Associated Press in May to be developing a tool similar to Google known as "Coc Coc," which means "Knock, Knock" in English. In a statement, Google said it welcomed the competition Coc Coc represented, according to the AP report. Local bloggers reported Nguyen Minh Triet, the son of Prime Minister Nguyen Tan Dung and a ranking member of the Communist Youth Union, was working to develop a local social media network to compete with, or possibly replace, Facebook.

Nguyen Anh Tuan, a legal activist who tracks local laws governing the Internet, believes the government has strong incentive to shut down Facebook as a platform for online journalism. He cites a case when local bloggers used Facebook to report news not covered in mainstream media of three children who were killed by tainted vaccines produced by a state-owned company. Follow-up investigative reports posted on blogs revealed that some 20 children had died from the same vaccine since 2010 without the government taking responsibility.

In an unprecedented online response, more than 10,000 Vietnamese social media users signed a petition on Facebook calling for the Minister of Health's resignation over the deaths. "The government sees danger in blogs and Facebook pages that allow people to comment and trade ideas," Tuan said. "Today they call for the resignation of the min-ister of health, tomorrow the prime minister or the entire Communist Party—that's what they think. If allowed to continue it will happen. . . . That's why they feel they need Decree 72 to control the Internet."

The conviction of Dinh Nhat Uy on October 29 was the first of a blogger or dissident specifically for using Facebook, news reports said. Uy had used the social media site to campaign for his brother's release from prison, where he is serving a four-year sentence on anti-state pro-paganda charges.

Many independent bloggers are motivated by a sense of injustice in Vietnamese society and the mainstream media's persistent failure to report on issues of import. Thang says he left a career in government service to become a full-time blogger in protest of rampant bribery and embezzlement of state funds at the civil engineering agency where he worked. "Local officials cooperated with private property developers to evict farmers and degrade the environment," said Thang, recounting his days as a civil servant. "I couldn't bear it, so I left my job."

Since 2007, Thang says, he has specialized in reporting and filming cases of villagers' being evicted from their lands to make way for state or state-linked development projects. This is a politically sensitive topic that pits grassroots people against the power of the party and is often censored or slanted in favor of the state in mainstream media coverage. Thang says he has also made several undercover visits to prisons and re-education camps to gather information and report on the condition of imprisoned political dissidents and fellow bloggers.

Bloggers in Vietnam support themselves financially in a variety of ways. Some work as registered journalists for government media and moonlight anonymously as bloggers; others contribute paid pieces to collective dissident blogs hosted outside Vietnam; still others rely on private businesses or property to support their blogging.

■ ■ ■

Thang is at the forefront of a movement that aims to train young blog-gers at underground locations how to report safely in a hostile environ-ment. Because independent bloggers lack proper press credentials, they often must blend in with the crowd at news events. One tactic he advises for protecting sensitive film footage: Thang always keeps a pocket full of decoy memory cards and frequently changes his active card, which he hands off to fellow undercover bloggers to spirit away in case of being abruptly searched or detained by the police or plainclothes officials.

As government harassment and threats against bloggers have inten-sified, Thang said, he has come under pressure from his family mem-bers to cease blogging. He believes the only reason he has avoided prison on trumped-up anti-state charges is because his uncle is a high-ranking member of the Communist Party–dominated National Assembly. Thang says he titled his blog "Man without a family name" in overt rejection of his family's Communist Party links.

The imprisonment and harsh harassment of certain critical blog-gers while others are treated more leniently has often stoked suspicions of state infiltration of underground blogging communities. But as the number of imprisoned and physically abused bloggers continues to rise, there are new signs of unity among bloggers who share a common cause in fighting back against the government's use of draconian anti-state laws to silence their voices.

In June, a group of bloggers started an online petition calling for the repeal of Article 258, a vague and arbitrary law that bans "abusing democratic freedoms." The call was in response to the arrests of two bloggers under the law's provision against "abusing democratic freedoms" as well as government suppression of bloggers who tried to cover or participate in "human rights picnics" organized in several Vietnamese cities in May. More than 100 Vietnamese bloggers signed the petition with their real names and blog URLs, including several anonymous and pseudonymous bloggers who revealed their true identities for the first time.

Bloggers who spearheaded the campaign submitted the signed petition on July 31 to the United Nations' Office of the High Commissioner for Human Rights in Bangkok, an appeal that they hoped would block Vietnam's bid for a rotational seat on the U.N. Human Rights Council beginning in 2014. In mid-November, Vietnam was nonetheless awarded a seat on the council. Underscoring the risk of challenging state authority, Pham Doan Trang, one of the bloggers behind the petition, said government agents posted threatening messages about her over social media on the day she met with the U.N. representatives. Two other bloggers, Phuong Dun and Thao Chi, were briefly detained by the authorities on August 5 upon their return to Hanoi from Bangkok.

"The higher profile we are, the more dangerous it is," Trang said in an interview with CPJ soon after handing the petition to the U.N. Trang, who has lived outside Vietnam since January 2013, said the authorities frequently question her family about her whereabouts while neighborhood friends have been recruited by state agents to inform on her. "It's a type of psychological warfare, pressuring relatives and friends. These are the risks all Vietnamese bloggers face for being too vocal."

*Shawn W. Crispin* is CPJ's senior Southeast Asia representative. He is the author of CPJ's 2012 report, "Vietnam's Press Freedom Shrinks Despite Open Economy."

# 6

# LEGACIES ON THE LINE

# Mandela's Legacy of Media Freedom Stands Its Ground

## By Sue Valentine

**People march to South Africa's parliament in protest of the Protection of Information Bill in Cape Town in 2011.**

*Source:* AP/Schalk van Zuydam.

In 2002, as South Africa's Institute for the Advancement of Journalism was celebrating its 10th anniversary, Anton Harber, co-founder and former editor of the *Weekly Mail*, was in line waiting to meet the guest of honor, the late Nelson Mandela.

As Harber approached, Mandela, then 83, looked puzzled, as if trying to remember Harber's face from a previous meeting. The editor extended his hand and introduced himself. "Anton Harber, Mr. Mandela," he said. "Ah, you remember me," Mandela exclaimed, displaying his broad, trademark grin.

There are countless stories of Mandela's grace and charm, which he used to good effect during South Africa's fraught political transition in 1994 and during his single five-year term as the first democratically elected president of South Africa. Mandela died on December 5, 2013. A free and vibrant press is one of his many cherished legacies.

Today, almost 20 years on, press freedom in South Africa remains entrenched in the constitution, enjoys the protection of the courts, and is supported by a dynamic civil society as the country prepares for its fifth democratic election in 2014.

Yet, it is precisely the unrelenting media exposure of corruption, poor service delivery, and destabilizing poverty that has needled the African National Congress, the ruling party, ever since apartheid gave way to majority rule.

Even while Mandela was championing press freedom, the challenges of governing a fractious and still polarized society gave him pause. That tension between ideals and the realities of governing has become even more pronounced during the ANC's continued monopoly on power.

Today under President Jacob Zuma's administration, political rhetoric critical of the news media has hardened, an instinct for secrecy is on the rise, and Zuma himself, both before taking office and as president, has been quick to threaten newspapers, columnists, and cartoonists with court action. There is legislation under consideration in Parliament that could restrict what is still the freest press in Africa. And, in some quarters, champions of "good news" are emerging, favoring positive stories to counter the litany of news about government failures, corruption and self-serving politicians.

The question is how deep are the roots of democracy planted two decades ago and how robust are the institutional safeguards that underpin the vision Mandela extolled of a strong and independent media?

Among South African citizens there is a "sustained demand for democracy," according to Afrobarometer, an independent research project that measures social, political, and economic sentiments in African countries. But when it comes to media freedom, the results are more mixed. A healthy majority of 70 percent agreed that the media should continue to investigate corruption, up from only half of the population in 2008. However, the study found that while 60 percent of South Africans believe that the media have a right to publish without government control, this is down from almost 80 percent in 2008. The number of people believing that the government has the right to prevent the media from publishing things that "might harm the society" has doubled, from 16 percent to 33 percent.

"South Africans may not be willing to go out on a limb if control of information is presented to them as a positive thing," said Paul Graham, an adviser to Afrobarometer. While the Right2Know civil society coalition launched in 2010 has been effective, it is an "elite campaign" Graham said. "There is no doubt that we are poised between Russia and China, and Brazil and India," referring to South Africa's membership in the group of emerging economies known as BRICS. "This is not to say we aren't free. We are much better off than we were, but we could become more autocratic and have our civil liberties more restricted than we expect."

■ ■ ■

In the days of apartheid, the ruling National Party used the hateful Internal Security Act of 1982, which was based on 1950s legislation, to crush freedom of expression and association. It banned newspapers, detained journalists, and censored information deemed to "endanger the security of the state or the maintenance of public order."

Four conglomerates, representing mining companies and business interests, owned all of the mainstream press. While some journalists and editors at these titles opposed apartheid, the owners supported the status quo, either actively or passively. They also controlled their own printing and distribution networks. Broadcasting was entirely state-controlled; the South African Broadcasting Corporation (SABC) held a monopoly of the airwaves and served as a propaganda arm of the government, broadcasting in 11 languages.

In the 1980s, when the white minority still ruled, the "alternative" press, such as the *Weekly Mail, New Nation, South,* and *Vrye Weekblad,* took the lead in exposing apartheid's brutality. Most relied on the support of international donors.

As the country's first democratic elections approached in 1994, Mandela—in one of his most frequently quoted speeches—told the International Press Institute in Cape Town:

> A critical, independent, and investigative press is the lifeblood of any democracy. The press must be free from state interference. It must have the economic strength to stand up to the blandishments of government officials. It must have sufficient independence from vested interests to be bold and inquiring without fear or favor. . . . It is only such a free press that can temper the appetite of any government to amass power at the expense of the citizen. . . . The African National Congress has nothing to fear from criticism. I can promise you, we will not wilt under close scrutiny. It is our considered view that such criticism can only help us to grow, by calling attention to those of our actions and omissions which do not measure up to our people's expectations and the democratic values to which we subscribe.

However, Mandela did not always support freedom of the media. In 1996, his criticism, especially of black journalists and editors he viewed as disloyal, set off alarm bells among press freedom advocates. In June 1997, Mandela met members of the South African National Editors Forum in a tense stand-off. According to excerpts from the exchange published in the *Rhodes Journalism Review,* Mandela charged that black journalists did not write freely because to earn a living they had to "please their white editors." Mandela also complained that editors "suppressed" ANC responses to critical articles.

The editor of the *Sowetan* at the time, Mike Siluma, questioned Mandela's emphasis on race, arguing that the focus should be on the role of media in a democracy. "You can genuinely change the color of owners, and the publications will not automatically see eye-to-eye with government, because there will still be disagreements—as there ought to be—when the need arises. We lose the bigger picture when we get obsessed by the racial one," he wrote in the *Rhodes Journalism Review.*

Yet both of Mandela's presidential successors have bridled consistently against press criticism, arguing that the country's newspapers in particular are biased against the ANC.

Thabo Mbeki, in the mid-1990s before becoming president, accused the press of "harboring a tendency to look for crises . . . faults and mistakes." According to Mbeki's biographer, Mark Gevisser, "By September 1995, Mbeki was branding any media criticism of the ANC as racist."

After being elected president in 1999, Mbeki initiated in 2001 an online weekly letter entitled *ANC Today* to counter what he perceived as hostile media. "The serious chilling effect Mbeki had on the media was to play the race card," said Gevisser. "He went for his critics—black and white—and demonized them, branding black critics 'Uncle Toms.' "

It was only in late 2007, when the ANC replaced Mbeki with Zuma as leader of the party, that the organization adopted a resolution to investigate the possible creation of a Media Appeals Tribunal. Rhetoric continued to heat up: An ANC spokesman, Jackson Mthembu, told journalists in July 2010 that they deserved to be punished if found guilty by a media tribunal. "If you have to go to prison, let it be," Mthembu said. "If you have to pay millions for defamation, let it be. If journalists have to be fired because they don't contribute to the South Africa we want, let it be."

An ANC discussion paper prepared in September 2010 said a cursory scan of the print media "reveals an astonishing degree of dishonesty, lack of professional integrity, and lack of independence" and cited "growing conglomeration of ownership and homogenization of content."

In 2011, amid growing calls by ANC members for the creation of a media tribunal by Parliament, press owners together with the South African National Editors Forum set up a Press Freedom Commission, including nine members from outside the media, chaired by a retired constitutional court judge.

The commission's report in April 2012 concluded that an independent regulatory mechanism would best serve press freedom. It said a majority of the Press Council of South Africa should be made up of representatives of the public; ethical standards should be strengthened and backed by a hierarchy of penalties, and public access to the council should be improved. The ANC welcomed this report, but it has not called off the possibility of a parliamentary investigation of the print media.

■ ■ ■

Despite ANC criticism of the press, only Zuma, both before his election as president and since, has brought legal action against the media. Between 2006 and 2010, Zuma took court action in 15 cases—suing newspapers, a radio station, cartoonists, a columnist, op-ed writers, and other journalists.

In October 2012, days before the case came to court, Zuma dropped one of his most prominent claims—a US$500,000 defamation suit against the cartoonist "Zapiro," a.k.a. Jonathan Shapiro. Zapiro's 2008 cartoon accused Zuma of manipulating the judicial system to fend off charges of corruption, and depicted him preparing to rape Lady Justice, who was being held down by key political allies who had helped Zuma topple Mbeki as head of the ANC at its 2007 party congress. (In 2006 Zuma had been charged with rape and acquitted.)

By May 2013, Zuma had dropped all outstanding cases against the media. His spokesman said that given the challenges facing the country, Zuma had decided he "must give way." A news report noted the decision might also have been influenced by the fact that Zuma's legal team missed a deadline for submitting legal documents for six claims against media houses and individuals.

The judiciary, meanwhile, has consistently defended media freedom as politicians and big business have resorted to civil courts to block publication or to sue. However, the approval of the Protection of State Information Bill by Parliament in April 2013 is the most tangible threat yet to a free press.

Having met fierce resistance, the "secrecy bill," as it was dubbed by its opponents, has been significantly improved since it was first introduced in 2008. But in its current form it continues to threaten journalists' watchdog role with jail terms of up to 25 years by not providing a public interest defense for anyone who discloses classified information "with the purpose of revealing corruption or other criminal activity."

In mid-September 2013, almost six months after the bill's approval by Parliament, Zuma announced that it "did not pass constitutional muster" and sent it back to Parliament. An ad hoc committee conducted a cursory review, making minor technical changes, but the ANC majority in the committee refused to review the bill more broadly. In November, Parliament adopted this version of the bill and returned it to Zuma to sign into law. The president could sign it or submit the bill to the constitutional court for review. If the bill is signed, a range of organizations is poised to bring a court challenge.

"We may win this round," former *Sunday Times* editor and political commentator Mondli Makhanya told CPJ, "but the bigger threat is the prevailing culture within the ANC, which is anti–freedom of expression and openness." He said the current ANC leadership was not instilling the values of the constitution among its members, but rather the opposite, painting the media as the opposition, even "the enemy."

While the introduction of the Protection of State Information bill arose from a legitimate need to redraft apartheid-era legislation, this urgency has been selectively applied. In response to press revelations in September 2012 of an upgrade to Zuma's private residence in Nkandla at a cost to taxpayers of US$25 million, the government was quick to invoke a notorious national security law, the National Key Points Act of 1980, to keep the property off limits to public discussion. Declaring Zuma's homestead a "national key point" has restricted further media inquiry.

Jovial Rantao, editor of the *Sunday Tribune*, says that while politicians claim to respect freedom of expression and the media, constant vigilance is required because of laws like the National Key Points Act and the secrecy bill and a failed attempt to introduce pre-publication screening for newspapers through an amendment to the Film and Publications Act. "We've been pushing back against the ANC for the best part of the last decade," Rantao told CPJ. "We have these guarantees on the books, but we dare not sleep on the job. We have to make sure that none of these inimical laws are snuck in under the radar."

Rantao, who is also chairman of the Southern African Editors' Forum, noted that while South African journalists face some challenges, these are "vastly different" from other countries in the region where "our colleagues deal with very serious situations."

■ ■ ■

After two decades of ANC power, the party has "good cause" to accuse the press of failing to reform, according to Libby Lloyd, a former South African journalist and now a researcher on freedom of expression and media policy. She cites 2011 parliamentary hearings into print media showing black ownership of the press at 14 percent, while female representation at board level was 4.4 percent. However, the demography of newsrooms has changed: 65 percent of editors heading mainstream publications were black in 2011, compared with 7 percent in 1994, according to the same parliamentary hearings.

Donors supporting independent newspapers redirected their funds after 1994. A decade into South Africa's democracy, only the *Weekly Mail* survived. An injection of support from the London *Guardian* in the 1990s led to its rebranding as the *Mail & Guardian*. Smaller, regional publications now struggle to compete against the conglomerates.

The most dramatic change in South Africa's media landscape since apartheid came through re-regulation of the airwaves. The current broadcasting environment, described in a report by Lloyd, includes some 200 community radio stations, five community television channels, 20 commercial radio stations, one national free-to-air private television channel, and digital pay television. The SABC remains the biggest news operation in the country with a mandate to provide news, education, and entertainment to all South Africans, but it has been plagued by financial mismanagement and executive interference in editorial practices.

A recent development on the South Africa media landscape has been the emergence of two news outlets privately owned by Indian investors with close ties to Zuma and with a declared commitment to "celebrate" South African achievements. The business interests of brothers Ajay, Atul, and Rajesh Gupta, who immigrated to South Africa in the 1990s, according to news reports, are divided into two parent companies operating in the information and technology sector and in mining. The family lives on a large estate in an established

Johannesburg suburb that has provoked controversy over its size. Unpacking the family's business interests has proved difficult due to a complex web of cross holdings and directorships, news reports say.

In 2010 the Gupta family launched the *New Age* newspaper. They are joint owners of Africa News Network 7, a pay-TV channel launched in August 2013. Zuma toured its studio days before its first broadcast. One of ANN7's new talk show hosts, Jimmy Manyi, a former government spin doctor, said "people in this country are sick and tired of negative press," and that the channel was committed to reporting good news and promoting patriotism, according to news reports.

■ ■ ■

The SABC's acting chief operations officer, Hlaudi Motsoeneng, provoked derision when he echoed this sentiment in August, telling a newspaper that 70 percent of the broadcaster's South African news content should focus on "good news." In September, Zuma told journalism students visiting Cape Town that media owners had a responsibility to reflect a "balanced view" of the country and not to dwell on negative news.

"Every time the media expose another scandal, we see a ratcheting up of pressure to be patriotic," *City Press* editor Ferial Haffajee told CPJ. In her view, the ultimate form of patriotism is to be a "critical patriot," but without jingoism and nationalism. "It is patriotic to expose corruption, to show the impact of waste and poor governance," she said.

"Bad news for the government is not necessarily bad news for the country. It all depends on how you look at it," Janet Heard, the head of news and assistant editor at the *Cape Times*, told CPJ. "Exposing corruption and ensuring better services can be considered good news."

Heard said media freedom in South Africa has been hard-won and is jealously guarded, but there are "warning bells" from the government. "The tone of finger-pointing is sharper, the secrecy bill shows a desire to silence and shut down," she said.

"All we can do is to continue what we've been doing and keep pushing the envelope," said Makhanya, the former *Sunday Times* editor, underscoring the country's strong institutional safeguards and the fact that the courts not only have ruled in favor of the media but have also consistently interpreted the law in the light of the constitution and freedom of expression. "There will come a point when the ANC is no longer in power and we must create media freedom as a norm for whoever comes in after the ANC," he said.

For the time being, the South African media remains dynamic and determinedly free, protected by a growing body of jurisprudence and a vigilant civil society. Groups like the Right2Know, which emerged in direct response to the introduction of the secrecy bill, continue to galvanize efforts to develop a "democratic and open society." Despite appeals by politicians for a respectful, patriotic media that should highlight positive developments, most media outlets are defiantly independent, and investigative journalism is thriving.

More than a decade after his handshake with Mandela, Anton Harber, now head of the journalism school at the University of the Witwatersrand, observed in a *Business Day* column in December 2011: "All of this makes for a highly contested and rowdy democracy. There are some who fear that noisiness, and would prefer calm agreement and silent consent. But the lesson of post-colonial Africa has been that it is not argument and contestation we should fear, but its absence. That raucous and sometimes jarring noise is the sound of a healthy young democracy at work."

"Nelson Mandela taught us what a free society looked like," said Makhanya. "Even Mandela was challenged by the media, but he became one of our biggest defenders. We created this state of media freedom for ourselves, now it's about defending it. We must do what we do and not be frightened."

*Sue Valentine*, *CPJ's Africa program coordinator, has worked as a journalist in print and radio in South Africa since the late 1980s, including at* The Star *newspaper in Johannesburg and as the executive producer of a national daily current affairs radio show on the SABC, South Africa's public broadcaster.*

# Hassan Rouhani and the Hope for More Freedom in Iran

*By D. Parvaz*

In his early months in office, Iranian President Hassan Rouhani, pictured in Tehran June 17, 2013, focused primarily on foreign affairs.

*Source:* Reuters/Fars News/Majid Hagdost.

Anyone focused on the June 2013 presidential campaign in Iran probably noticed two things: The winner, President Hassan Rouhani, courted the youth and reformist vote before the actual reformist, Mohamed Reza Aref, dropped out, and Rouhani used social media, in English and Farsi, to communicate, even though it is banned in Iran.

Since he took office on August 3, Rouhani has also built on comments he made during the televised debates about excessive controls forced on Iranians, especially in the areas of arts and media—references that appeared to close the door on eight years of Mahmoud Ahmadinejad's hard-line administration.

It's unclear how much power Rouhani has to change how Iran's press operates, assuming he genuinely desires reform, because Ayatollah Ali Khamenei, Iran's supreme leader, has final say and veto power. Nevertheless, there is an air of optimism and watchfulness in the country, where every small gesture is seen as a potential omen of greater freedom. Two factors that may work in favor of the press are the practical needs for liberalized communications technology and the continued engagement of young journalists.

"The red lines and censorship have eased, for no particular reason," said one reporter in Tehran who was awaiting trial on charges of threatening national security and who declined to be named. He noted that the same thing happened during reformist President Mohammad Khatami's time in office, and that journalists were working in a relatively "calm situation."

For instance, immediately after Rouhani was elected, while Ahmadinejad was still in office, Viber, a Voice over Internet Protocol application that provides access to the Internet, was unblocked.

And, in September, when Facebook and Twitter became accessible for a few hours, both were abuzz with word that things had changed. The access turned out to be a technical error, and both sites were blocked again, but the response was overwhelming and telling.

Iran strictly controls the entry and movement of foreign journalists within its borders, where press credentials can be revoked if the government is displeased with how something is reported. For example, in 2012, the Reuters news agency temporarily lost its press credentials in Iran after characterizing female martial artists as "assassins."

And in 2011, the government temporarily revoked the press credentials of 11 foreign correspondents for reporting on anti-government protests. There was little reporting and complaint on this issue by the news organizations involved because they feared not getting their credentials back.

The U.S. at times plays a similar game with Iranian journalists, as CPJ Executive Director Joel Simon pointed out in *Foreign Policy* magazine, with few visas being granted for Iranian reporters, and those who are admitted generally restricted within a 25-mile radius of U.N. headquarters. Simon urges an end to what he described as the "Cold War-era" constraints both countries are placing on each other's journalists.

"Based on what he has said about opening up the academic scene and his appointment of a competent lady as his [vice-president] for Women and Family Affairs, it is not farfetched that Rouhani will also seek to loosen up on the crackdowns," said Mehrzad Boroujerdi, the president of the International Society for Iranian Studies and the director of the Middle Eastern Studies Program at Syracuse University. "I expect fewer charges filed against journalists, more licenses issued to reformist news outlets, less censorship of books and newspapers."

Even within the limited framework of presidential powers, there are changes that Rouhani could make—or at least push for—that would dramatically alter Iran's media landscape. With opposition outlets routinely censored or shut down, and only a handful of major reformist newspapers, such as *Shargh* and *Etemad*, still operating, the terrain now is barren except for state news agencies and hard-line publications. Even officially approved newspapers and websites are subject to periodic bans and shutdowns.

Well-known reporters such as Mohammad Davari and Masoud Bastani, both among those arrested after the disputed 2009 presidential elections, remain technically under arrest while being granted occasional furloughs (in Davari's case, after suffering a heart attack upon hearing of his brother's death).

The International Campaign for Human Rights in Iran has prepared an extensive roadmap that offers Rouhani realistic suggestions, ones that focus on changes he could make at the ministerial and legislative levels.

"The best place to start is to put in place infrastructural protections for press freedom, so that not only under Rouhani would the situation improve, but beyond him, so they are not specific to his government," said Hadi Ghaemi, executive director of the New York-based rights group.

Introducing legislation on press freedom that explicitly defines and protects free speech would be crucial, as would Ministry of Labor regulations allowing independent associations representing the interests of journalists (something that has been under attack since the journalists association was shut down in 2009 and has not been allowed to function since).

The roadmap also suggests that permits for publishing newspapers and press credentials for local and foreign journalists be granted without consideration of political views. Government agencies should be prevented from filing lawsuits against media outlets and journalists who report critically on the state. "They need to promote a culture of tolerance of criticism," Ghaemi said.

Ghaemi also complains that far too many ministries have a hand in media control and censorship, making it impossible to keep track of the standards and practices that journalists are expected to maintain. Though the media fall under the control of the Ministry of Culture and Islamic Guidance (simply referred to as "ershad," or guidance, in Farsi), reporters, editors and bloggers are arrested by the judiciary. Meanwhile, the Ministry of Intelligence plays both surveillance and censorship games with the press.

"This is why we need legislation which would overall define the boundaries of press freedoms according to the constitution and international obligations," Ghaemi said. "One ministry that certainly interferes with the working press, even though it is not within its mandate, is the Ministry of Intelligence, which regularly outlines what is allowed to be published and what is not allowed to be published to editors."

Complicating matters further is that it is not simply a matter of what is reported or published, but how the state chooses to interpret it.

A CPJ special report showed that in the lead-up to the 2013 elections, at least 40 journalists were imprisoned in Iran. Most were charged with either "spreading propaganda against the state," "acting against national security," or "insulting the supreme leader." Given Iran's pattern of rotating critical journalists in and out of prison, and the difficulty of confirming the motives behind a journalists' detention, it's possible that more are incarcerated. In March, the Ministry of

Intelligence announced that 600 Iranian journalists were believed to be part of an anti-state network.

Any efforts by Rouhani to end intimidation of the media could fail, as Syracuse University's Boroujerdi points out.

"A great deal will depend on what Rouhani accomplishes on the foreign policy front. If he is successful, then he will have the necessary political capital to take on the conservatives on a range of domestic issues including press freedom," Boroujerdi said.

"However, his failure on the foreign policy front will embolden the conservatives to torpedo his domestic initiatives as a way of discrediting him. Rouhani and his people have learned from the experience of Khatami and will try to avoid the mistakes he made," Boroujerdi said. "By the same token I don't think he will be as brazen as Khatami on the media freedom issue."

Even when Khatami tried to cleanse the Ministry of Intelligence of those who focused on the press, some of those individuals ended up in what Ghaemi described as "parallel institutions" close to the supreme leader, where they were still able to exert influence.

For example, the reformist journalist Akbar Ganji was imprisoned during Khatami's administration because his reporting on a series of political killings threatened the positions of several hard-liners linked to the Ministry of Intelligence.

During Ahmadinejad's administration, even hard-line journalists loyal to him were detained. The arrest of his media adviser, Ali Akbar Javanfekr, who was apprehended in 2011 by security officers representing the judiciary, shows just how out of the president's reach such matters can be.

■ ■ ■

The hope for better conditions is not an abstraction. Reporters working in Iran, which CPJ ranked as the fourth-most-censored country in the world in 2012, continually risk their liberty and even their lives. Detention, investigation, and criminal charges are routine.

One reporter, willing to talk only on condition of anonymity for fear of reprisal, described reporting during Ahmadinejad's two terms in office in stark terms.

"We worked for eight years in hell," she said, detailing years of reporting in fear, watching her colleagues go into exile, and knowing that if she ever left her country, she might never be able to return—an unacceptable sacrifice.

A respected veteran who reported for more than a decade for various print publications—some shut down by the government—she was arrested and held in solitary confinement. She spoke while out on bail and barred from leaving the country, awaiting a court date on charges of spreading anti-government propaganda, which is punishable by up to one year in prison.

The reporter said she has hope for a better legal process under the government, but little hope for a freer press. "Even during Khatami's government, many of the journalists, such as Akbar Ganji, Abbas Abdi, Ahmad Zaidabadi, Alireza Eshraghi, and many more were in jail," she said.

Things were worse under Ahmadinejad, she said, when "more journalists were in jail, especially after the 2009 election," when street protests over the contested results set loose a campaign of repression that did not let up for four years.

The reporter pointed to the many Iranian journalists forced into exile for fear of lengthy jail sentences—or worse, as in the case of blogger Sattar Beheshti, who, the authorities said, "died of shock" on November 3, 2012, his fifth day in custody. He was never charged with a crime and never set foot in a court.

In a recorded Skype conversation with a friend shortly before his detention and death, Beheshti spoke of leaving the country, worrying that his elderly mother would not be able to tolerate the strain of his arrest.

Although he said he couldn't understand why his notebooks had been confiscated by the authorities, as they contained nothing controversial, Beheshti seemed resigned to the worst.

"If they want to throw a noose around my neck," Beheshti said, "I'd say that there's honor in this death compared to the shame of this life." Family members were not allowed to view his body and opposition media reported they were attacked by plainclothes security men at a memorial service for him.

■  ■  ■

Censorship is not new to Iran and was imposed long before the establishment of the Islamic Republic in 1979. Successive regimes have maintained tight control not only over what is published and broadcast but also over the flow of information, how information is communicated.

For example, in February 2012, more than a dozen reporters were arrested, with warrants issued for many more, not because of what they had reported, but because of their contact with foreign media.

Iran's censors also have a reputation of keeping up with new technologies. Social media tools such as Facebook and Twitter are blocked and banned, accessible within the country only via Virtual Private Networks. Surprisingly, however—while officials have never acknowledged it—all presidential candidates in the 2013 race had Twitter and Facebook accounts. Rouhani still has one, @HassanRouhani, which tweets in English. In September, Twitter verified the account of Mohammad Javad Zarif, Iran's foreign minister, even though his tweets are not legally accessible to those inside the country.

Jillian York, director for international freedom of expression at the Electronic Frontier Foundation, a nonprofit watchdog for digital rights based in San Francisco, suggested this should not be viewed as a signal that restrictions on such media are about to be lifted. However, she said, "it shows that there's an understanding of how organizing and politics will work in the future, and if the authorities have any success in using those tools, then hopefully, they'll be able to see the benefit of keeping the Internet open enough for communication with the rest of the world."

York described Iran as being "on par with China" when it comes to digital freedom, particularly because both countries make a point of going after tools intended to protect privacy. "They're the best at keeping one step ahead of Internet users," she said. "The blocking of websites is quick, often for a particular time to coincide with a particular event or an election."

York said she hoped that Rouhani would at least take steps to ensure access to communication technology—if not for the sake of a free press, then for other more pragmatic reasons. "While blocking political speech is terrible, the blocking of communication technologies does more to inhibit the educational and economic growth of the nation," she said. She added that the lifting of some U.S. sanctions on Iran has also eased the crippling effect on some communications technologies.

Akbar Ganji, a veteran journalist who lives in exile in the U.S., expects Rouhani to "pursue increased freedoms for media and political parties," he said. But, while he expects improvement compared with Ahmadinejad's time in office, Ganji, who spent years in prison under a reformist president, added, "It's unlikely to be as good as the time of the reformists. The hard-liners are holding strong to ensure that that era is not repeated."

In his first months in office, Rouhani focused primarily on foreign affairs. He reached out to the West, particularly Washington, not only via social media, but also at the United Nations and by granting interviews and writing an opinion column in *The Washington Post* calling for measured negotiations with the U.S. And there were genuine signs of change in Iran: In September, the authorities freed 11 political prisoners, including Nasrin Sotoudeh, a celebrated rights lawyer who represented activists and journalists and was serving a six-year prison sentence for "threatening national security."

Meanwhile, Ghaemi, head of the International Campaign for Human Rights in Iran, said the pool of young journalists willing to come forward has not yet run dry in Iran, where the government has failed to create a press corps "confined to regime loyalists."

These journalists are the ones who keep getting arrested, keep getting released and keep on writing, again and again. "No matter how many waves of arrests, detentions and harassment of journalists we've had, which have landed many in jail, hundreds of them fleeing the country, journalism remains a very essential part of Iranian society in terms of continuing to produce new journalists who refuse to be silenced," Ghaemi said.

*D. Parvaz, a reporter and special projects editor, works for Al-Jazeera English and is based in Doha, Qatar.*

# Violence and Judicial Censorship Mar Brazil's Horizon

*By Carlos Lauría*

**Brazilian President Dilma Rousseff has created a working group to study the issue of attacks against journalists, but concrete steps have been inadequate, journalists say.**

*Source*: AP/Eraldo Peres.

**B**razilian authorities, piqued by revelations of U.S. spying, rushed to offer protection for American reporter Glenn Greenwald, who lives in Brazil, after he revealed details of U.S. National Security Agency surveillance activities in the country.

The Brazilian Senate quickly began an official investigation into allegations, leaked to Greenwald by former NSA contractor Edward Snowden, that the American spy agency even intercepted President Dilma Rousseff's personal communications. To register her anger at the Obama administration, Rousseff postponed a planned October 23 state visit to the United States and later denounced the spying at the United Nations General Assembly.

The government's proclaimed concern for the safety of an American journalist then reporting for *The Guardian* of London, however, stands in sharp contrast to the dismal performance of Latin America's largest country in protecting its own reporters from violence or ridding the country of its onerous criminal defamation laws.

Brazil has seen a sharp rise in the number of journalists killed with impunity in recent years, making it one of the most dangerous countries for reporters in the world. At least four journalists were killed in 2013, three of them in direct retaliation for their journalism.

In addition to this climate of violence, journalists and press freedom advocates have identified judicial censorship as the second-most-critical problem affecting Brazilian reporters and media outlets. In the past five years, hundreds of lawsuits have been filed by political figures, government officials, and businessmen, alleging that critical journalists have damaged their reputation or invaded their privacy, CPJ research shows. The practice has become so common that it is known as the "industry of compensation." Plaintiffs usually seek court orders to bar journalists from publishing anything further about them and to have existing online material deleted.

News outlets and journalists are often subject to intimidation in the form of multiple lawsuits, straining their financial resources and forcing them to halt their criticism. Lower court judges often admit such lawsuits into court, eventually ruling against the press, CPJ research shows. These rulings are often revoked on appeal, but, by then, the financial damage has been done and information has been censored.

Rousseff, a former Marxist rebel who fought against the military regime in the 1960s and is up for re-election in 2014, has promised reforms and has created a working group to study the issue of attacks against journalists. Concrete measures have been both inadequate and ineffective, journalists and human rights activists told CPJ.

"Even though Brazilian authorities have identified violence as one of the problems affecting press freedom, efforts to address this issue have been clearly insufficient," said Celso Schroder, president of the National Federation of Journalists, known as FENAJ.

Beyond the death toll in 2013, four journalists were killed for their work in 2012 and three others in 2011. As a result, for the second consecutive year, Brazil appeared on CPJ's Impunity Index, which calls attention to countries where journalists are frequently murdered and the killers go free.

A total of 27 journalists have been killed in direct reprisal for their work in Brazil since 1992, CPJ research shows. Nine of the 10 journalists killed for their work in the past three years had reported on official corruption or crime, and all but one worked in provincial areas.

Brazil's official reaction to the spike in violence against the news media—not unlike its response to widespread street protests in 2013 over rising public transport costs, political corruption, crime, and the government's lavish spending on sports stadiums for the 2014 World Cup and 2016 Olympics—has been mainly rhetorical.

Federal Human Rights Minister Maria do Rosário Nunes established a working group in March 2013 aimed at discussing violence against reporters, referring cases to the appropriate authorities, and following up on judicial investigations. Its members—several civil society groups, representatives from the presidency, and the communications and justice ministries—met several times throughout the year.

The idea, according to do Rosário, is to "evaluate and assess risks for journalists under threat and create a monitoring system that can effectively track free press violations." Do Rosário, who reports to the president, acknowledged that the situation for reporters working in isolated areas is dire. Victoria Balthar de Souza Santos, a spokeswoman in her office, told CPJ that the group is seriously considering a permanent watchdog unit to monitor threatened journalists.

A member of the working group, Article 19, a U.K.-based organization that champions free speech, has recommended creating a federal program to protect threatened journalists in imminent danger, according to Paula Martins, Article 19's director in South America. Risk evaluation and protective measures would be decided by a group composed of members of civil society with expertise on press issues, freedom of expression, and human rights, Martins said.

If created, Brazilian officials told CPJ, the program would replicate one currently in place since 2004 for the protection of human rights advocates. That program provides assistance, including relocation and police protection, for those who have received serious threats or feel under attack for their work. While this program has assisted a number of human rights activists, it still has several problems, according to Martins. "It lacks resources, there is not much official information available to the public, and there are serious coordinating problems between the states and the federal government," she said.

A similar protection program in Colombia is often cited for helping to reduce violence against journalists. In Colombia, a committee of government officials and civil society representatives meets frequently to assess the security needs of journalists under threat. In some cases, the government arranges direct protection, including security guards, while in other cases it supports such tactics as relocation. Though hardly flawless, the program has assisted numerous journalists under threat and prevented physical attacks against Colombian reporters, according to CPJ research.

One of Brazil's leading investigative journalists, Mauri König, who writes for the daily *Gazeta do Povo* in Curitiba, said such a program is long overdue. "The government has taken too long to establish a protection mechanism, and in the meantime, journalists continue to be killed with impunity," he said.

■ ■ ■

The number of fatalities among journalists in recent years reflects the failure of the Rousseff administration to prevent them. Journalism is now a high-risk profession in Brazil, and impunity is still a problem despite sporadic progress made by Brazilian prosecutors. CPJ has documented convictions in at least six killings of journalists in recent years. In August 2013, for instance, João Francisco dos Santos was sentenced to 27 years in prison on charges of shooting and killing radio journalist and blogger Francisco Gomes de Medeiros in the northeastern city of Caicó, according to news reports. Gomes was shot at least five times in front of his home on October 18, 2010. Though the conviction is a step toward improving Brazil's deteriorating record on impunity, justice is sluggish: Some cases can drag on for years and only a few are ever solved, CPJ research shows.

Several journalists, legislators, and government officials believe that a project under consideration by Congress will speed cases through the judicial system. The bill would give federal police jurisdiction to investigate crimes against journalists when there is evidence of lapses or incompetence at the state level. The presidents of both chambers of Congress, Sen. Renan Calheiros and Deputy Henrique Alves, told CPJ they will support any measure to combat impunity in the cases of murdered journalists.

Two of the largest local press groups, FENAJ, and the Brazilian Press Association, known as ABI, representing editors and reporters throughout the country, back the proposal. "Investigations must rely on the hands of federal authorities," said FENAJ's Schroder, who believes federal police have more resources and are less corrupt. The Association of Brazilian Investigative Journalists, or ABRAJI, whose directors cannot reach consensus, has not endorsed the bill. Fernando Rodrigues, one of the group's directors and a prominent journalist with the daily *Folha de Sao Paulo*, believes the bill is not inclusive enough, because it fails to refer to the constitutional right to freedom of expression. Rodrigues said he fears it could be interpreted as a privilege for reporters at a time when everyone is threatened by escalating violence across the country. During ABRAJI's annual congress in October, Minister do Rosário said that federalization of crimes that violate human rights, including the murder of journalists, would help to combat impunity.

Article 19's Paula Martins said the bill may not be necessary, because a constitutional amendment approved in 2004 addresses grave human rights abuses. Constitutional Amendment 45 reformed more than 20 provisions of the Brazilian Constitution, establishing better judicial mechanisms to protect human rights, according to Martins.

The reforms amended Article 109, granting the Attorney General's Office the power to transfer a case to federal jurisdiction when grave human rights violations are suspected. Though no cases have been transferred to federal jurisdiction under this reform, in theory, federal prosecutors can invoke the amendment to investigate such cases.

Laura Tresca, Article 19's freedom of information officer in Brazil, said that in addition to the amendment, there is also legislation dating to 2002 that allows federal police to investigate crimes against journalists. While this is true, the legislation says federal authorities may intervene only once officials establish that the crime constitutes a human rights violation. Deputy Delegado Protógenes, a former federal police officer, presented the original proposal in April 2011 and said he would consider introducing changes to the bill in order to strengthen it and then steer it through the legislative process.

Another Latin American nation, Mexico, with an even worse record of violence against journalists, has adopted sweeping reform legislation to tackle its own problem. On May 3, Mexican President Enrique Peña Nieto signed legislation that enabled a constitutional amendment giving the federal government broader jurisdiction to prosecute crimes against freedom of expression.

With the amendment of Article 73 of the Mexican Constitution, federal authorities have jurisdiction over any crime against "journalists, people, or outlets that affects, limits, or impinges upon the right to information and freedom of expression and the press." The reform followed years of advocacy by CPJ and other press freedom groups, and is only one step toward bringing to justice the killers of Mexican journalists.

In soccer-crazed Brazil, even critical sports commentary can turn deadly, which is why one family is demanding justice through the courts while the proposed bill to expand federal police powers remains stalled in the Chamber of Deputies.

Valério Luiz de Oliveira, a reporter with Radio Jornal in the city of Goiânia, was shot to death by an unidentified gunman on a motorcycle in July 2012. Luiz was known for his criticism of the management of the local soccer team Atletico Goianiense, according to news reports. Before his death, he was barred from entering the team's headquarters. In February 2013, the authorities arrested the former vice president of the club, three members of the military police, and a butcher, all accused of involvement in the killing. The five suspects were released in May after an injunction filed by their lawyers. Then, in September, Valério Luiz Filho, the journalist's son, requested a federal court hearing before the state legislature in Goiânia, alleging that state authorities were incapable of solving the crime because of pressure and intimidation. As of early November 2013, his request remained unanswered.

■ ■ ■

The elimination of Brazil's infamous 1967 Press Law, enacted during military rule, by the Supreme Federal Tribunal in 2009 was hailed as a step forward in the campaign against restrictive defamation laws in the Americas. But journalists can still go to jail for their work. Different articles of the penal code (138, 139, and 140) stipulate a month to two years in prison for defamation and slander, with more severe penalties when the crime is committed against the president, or against the head of a foreign government, against a public official in the performance of his official duties, or against a person who is disabled or over 60 years old (Article 141).

Claims of defamation are clearly visible in Google's Transparency Report, which was released for the first time in 2009. It compiles requests from governments to remove content from the company's platforms. Brazil is ranked at the top of the list. During the second half of 2012, Google documented a surge in requests from Brazil, representing an increase of 265 percent compared with the previous reporting period. The main reason for the increase were the 2012 municipal elections. Almost half of the total requests called for the removal of 756 pieces of content related to alleged violations of the Brazilian Electoral Code, which forbids defamation and commentary that offends candidates. Google has appealed on the basis that the content is protected by freedom of expression under the Brazilian Constitution.

Local journalists believe that politicized decisions by the judiciary are hindering coverage of issues of national interest. "Censorship imposed by lower courts often limits press freedom and creates a climate of legal insecurity among journalists," said Mauri König, a 2012

CPJ International Press Freedom Award winner. On many occasions, he said, reporters avoid controversial issues fearing legal persecution.

But prominent members of the judiciary play down the threat. Chief Justice Joaquim Barbosa, as well as one of his predecessors, Antonio Cesar Peluso, each told CPJ that they do not believe that judicial censorship is a big issue, despite research by local and international groups that shows otherwise. Though both acknowledged that there have been instances in which plaintiffs who felt that their honor had been challenged or their privacy invaded have succeeded in blocking publication, they argue this does not represent a threat to press freedom in Brazil. Both said that freedom of expression guarantees in the constitution are strong enough and that judicial censorship cases are not widespread and do not pose a serious threat. When confronted with cases documented by human rights groups, they said that most of the decisions are later revoked on appeal. Both defended the independence of the Brazilian judiciary.

■ ■ ■

There is a melancholy aspect to modern-day Brazil that stands in contrast to its storied beaches, bossa nova rhythms, glorified soccer tradition, and the vibrant wilderness of the Amazonian rainforest. Economic inequality and extreme poverty, a crack-cocaine epidemic, human trafficking, and deadly violence are some of the country's various challenges. The violence against journalists and censorship are serious setbacks that have degraded the press freedom landscape and require a decisive government response. Without free and independent journalism to report on these shortcomings and spur public debate, it will be difficult to resolve them.

As the host of the 2014 FIFA World Cup and the 2016 Summer Olympics, Brazil expects to receive a major influx of tourists in the next few years. With millions of visitors crowding the world's fourth-largest democracy, and the fifth-most-populous nation, these issues will come under increased international scrutiny.

Responding to the massive protests in 2013, Rousseff tried to assure the world that Brazil is a peaceful nation. "Football and sport are symbols of peace and peaceful coexistence among peoples," she said in a nationally televised speech.

As Brazil's profile rises in concert with its global influence, the Rousseff administration believes 2014 will be a great opportunity to show off Brazil's rich culture. The president, who will be in the midst of the election campaign during the World Cup, knows that all eyes will be on Brazil. Journalists and free-speech advocates hope the government, shamed by the nation's poor record on press freedom, will take decisive action to address the threats to Brazil's media. "Unpunished violence against the press and judicial censorship will certainly damage the country's image before international public opinion," König said.

As the World Cup draws nearer, Brazil must go from rhetoric to action. Deadly violence against the press, impunity, and censorship, call into question Brazil's true commitment to democratic values and human rights.

*CPJ Senior Americas Program Coordinator **Carlos Lauría**, a native of Buenos Aires, is a widely published journalist who has written extensively for Noticias, the leading Spanish-language newsmagazine.*

# 7

# GETTING AWAY WITH MURDER

# When Journalists Are Killed, Witnesses May Be Next

*By Elisabeth Witchel*

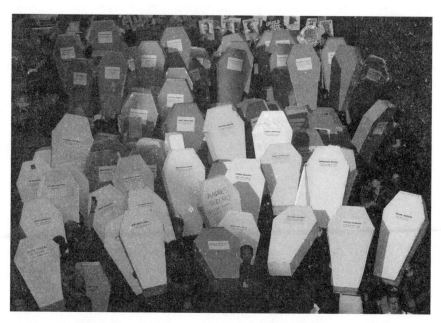

Filipino journalists and supporters in Manila brandish mock coffins at a rally to demand justice on the third anniversary of the killings of 32 journalists and media workers in Maguindanao in 2009.

*Source:* AP/Aaron Favila.

A s the day approached for Haider Ali to give his testimony at Anti-Terrorism Court III inside Karachi Central Prison, a venue chosen for security, it seemed a pivotal moment for Pakistan's journalists also neared.

Haider had identified four out of five suspects in police custody accused of carrying out the murder of Wali Khan Babar, a well-known television news presenter for Geo TV who was assassinated on his way home from work on January 13, 2011. Unlike the cases of nearly two dozen other journalists murdered for their work in Pakistan over the past decade, Babar's had progressed to a trial, and it offered a rare hope that the seemingly endless cycle of impunity and violence against Pakistan's press might finally come to a halt.

That hope was doused when, on the night of November 11, 2012, less than 48 hours before Haider would appear before the court, two unidentified men shot and killed him on the street outside the building where he was staying. The death of one of the last remaining known witnesses to Babar's murder—at least four others linked to the prosecution were previously killed, including witnesses, informants, and investigators—brought justice to a standstill. At the time of this writing, not one individual had been convicted of these crimes.

Killing witnesses has become an all too easy and effective method of stymying justice in the many cases of journalists murdered around the world. With poor standards for forensic evidence the norm in many countries where repeated targeted violence against journalists takes place, witness testimony is crucial to pursuing convictions. However, as was the case with Haider, the authorities often fail to grant witnesses adequate protection. Their stories also reveal something about those killers—thugs and masterminds who wield such immense power and influence that they are able to manipulate justice through corruption, violence, and fear.

"Babar's case can be a master script for any James Bond–like film or any movie on the underworld," said Mazhar Abbas, a prominent journalist in Pakistan who is the director of current affairs at Express News TV and a former secretary-general of the Pakistan Federal Union of Journalists. "And the way he was killed, and those directly or indirectly involved in the investigation, raised many questions."

In the past 10 years, 348 journalists have been murdered for their work worldwide. In only a handful of cases—one in 10—have any perpetrators been brought to trial and sentenced. The few and precious gains made in the fight against impunity are largely the product of the testimony of witnesses. But the risks are immense, and many pay dearly.

Some witnesses are courageous colleagues making immense sacrifices, such as Edgar Amoro, who was gunned down in 2005 after identifying the killers of fellow Philippine journalist Edgar Damalerio. Others are accused accomplices turned state witnesses, like Yuri Nesterov, injured in a grenade attack while under police escort in the Ukraine.

In the past four years, at least six witnesses in cases of murdered journalists have been killed along with at least eight others connected to investigations, including federal investigators looking into the case of Armando Rodriguez, who was shot in his car in Juarez, Mexico, in 2009. Add to this the threats that curtail, silence, or drive into exile other witnesses and the reach of intimidation is pervasive.

Nowhere are these elements more overtly in play than in the trial in the massacre at Ampatuan Town in the Philippines. At least 195 suspects have been charged, and dozens are still wanted for carrying out the 2009 ambush in Maguindanao province on the island of Mindanao. The victims, 58 in total, including 32 journalists and media workers, were slaughtered as they accompanied local politician Esmael Mangudadatu to submit his papers to run for governor against Andal Ampatuan Jr., son of the incumbent governor, Andal Ampatuan Sr. Their bodies were buried en masse with a backhoe.

Many expected that such ruthless, large-scale carnage would surely be a tipping point—a wake-up call for the Philippine government to prove its justice system is viable. Yet, four years later, there have been no convictions. The targeting of witnesses and family members has been a major factor behind this failure.

Suwaib Upham was the first key witness to the Maguindanao killings to be eliminated—shot and killed by an unidentified gunman on June 14, 2010, in Parang municipality, Maguindanao. Upham had been a militia member for the Ampatuan family, accused of perpetrating the massacre, and had agreed to testify in exchange for protection. According to Human Rights Watch, the Philippine Department of Justice was still considering his request for protection at the time of his killing. Several months before Upham's murder, two relatives of witnesses were killed and a third was injured after being shot multiple times. "Witnesses won't come forward if there is a 'second Maguindanao massacre' of witnesses and their families," Elaine Pearson, deputy Asia director of Human Rights Watch, said in a statement at the time.

Another wave of violence struck the trial in 2012. In May that year, the body of Esmael Amil Enog, an important prosecution witness, was found. The manner of his killing—he was hacked to pieces and stuffed into a bag—was viewed as a warning to others. Enog had testified the year before in a Manila court that another accomplice, Alijol Ampatuan, had ordered him to drive 36 militiamen to what turned out to be the site of the massacre.

Enog "is one of the very few witnesses with direct testimony as to the armed men who were present that day," said Prima Jesusa Quinsayas, a lawyer working for the Freedom Fund for Filipino Journalists in the Philippines, assisting families of victims as a private prosecutor. The Philippine justice system allows outside counsel to assist public prosecutors at the behest of victims or their families. "When he testified, not all accused had been arrested," Quinsayas said. "Enog was able to identify only four in court as the rest were not yet among those detained and arraigned."

Enog's testimony led prosecutors to seek Alijol Ampatuan as a state witness. They found him too late. His body was discovered in June that year.

"We feel worried for the security of the other witnesses, even for the security of our lawyers and the families of the victims," said Mary Grace Morales, whose husband and sister, both journalists, were among the 2009 Ampatuan victims. "What if all of our witnesses will be gone? Who will testify in court?" she said. "When all of those who witnessed the crimes are also dead, the trial will be useless. Justice will not be served."

The loss of witnesses is of particular concern for this trial, since forensic evidence is widely considered to be flawed. "The case would collapse if you rely on evidence," said Jose Pablo Baraybar, executive director of Equipo Peruano de Antropologia Forense (EPAF), a Peruvian-based NGO which promotes justice in cases of human rights abuses by providing forensic training and investigation services. He has conducted several training sessions for the Philippine police. "If you kill witnesses," he said, "then there is nothing."

Baraybar and a U.K. global security expert, Chris Cobb-Smith, who has investigated other cases involving killed journalists, went to the crime scene in Maguindanao at the behest of the National Human Rights Commission and other human rights groups. What he found resembled the scene of a natural disaster rather than Hollywood's CSI franchise. Families, national police, local police, the army, and other interested parties had trampled through the site with little coordination. "The whole thing was a mess," Baraybar said.

Basic equipment—refrigeration to preserve the bodies, cameras, mapping technology—was severely lacking. Cobb-Smith recalls borrowing a metal detector from his hotel's security guard. They found shells, dentures, and other key evidence that hadn't been picked up by the police. "As a result, the evidence has too many anomalies," Cobb-Smith said.

Insufficient resources and expertise to document human rights abuses is common in many countries. "It's a current theme among NGOs to concentrate on forensics. I get sent photographs weekly," said Cobb-Smith, who is often asked to evaluate evidence but finds it difficult because basic training hasn't been applied to its collection, such as documenting from which angles the photos were taken.

The murder of Wali Babar in Pakistan and the Ampatuan massacre in the Philippines are among the most dramatic cases of murdered journalists in the world. The deaths prompted domestic and international condemnation of both countries and their outrageous records of impunity.

Leaders in both countries have made public commitments to prosecute the killers, but if witnesses are so vital to successful convictions, how is it that, even in these cases where public pressure is weighty, the authorities fail to protect so many of them?

Both countries have the ability to guard witnesses in these cases. After Babar's murder in Pakistan, the Sindh High Court, the regional court of appeals for Karachi cases, ordered the provincial government to provide security for the witnesses as well as for the lawyers in the case. The order was in line with Pakistan's Anti-Terrorism Act of 1997, which requires the protection of judges, counsel, public prosecutors, witnesses, and other persons concerned with court proceedings.

The Philippines' system is more evolved, with an established witness protection program. Though criticized as severely lacking resources and prone to security lapses, it has yielded some successes. Under the leadership of prosecutor Leo Dacero, who died in 2010 in the early days of the Ampatuan trial, the protection program played a pivotal role in gaining convictions in the murders of two journalists, Edgar Damalerio and Marlene Garcia-Esperat.

But these government efforts are faltering in the face of the unchecked power wielded by the groups believed to be responsible. In a CPJ special report in 2013, journalist Elizabeth Rubin examined impunity in Pakistan's violence against the news media, including the case of Wali Babar Khan. Suspects arrested in Khan's murder are linked to the Muttahida Quami Movement (MQM), a political party that is the main heavyweight in Karachi's political turf wars, with influence among the police and the government and buttressed by an illegal armed wing.

Rubin's report suggests that an all-out assault against individuals connected to the investigation and prosecution of Babar's murder has been waged to keep the MQM beyond the reach of justice. The full extent of the violence employed over the past two years against those with a role to play in bringing Babar's killers to justice is truly shocking.

In addition to Haider, a police informant, Rajab Ali Bengali, was found dead in a sack within two weeks of the murder—and with him, a note naming head constable Arshad Kundi, the informant's handler, as the next victim. Just days later, two men on a motorcycle shot police constable Asif Rafiq, who had been on the scene of Babar's murder and identified the killers' vehicle. Kundi was soon after killed in another drive-by motorcycle attack. The brother of Police Chief Shafiq Tanoli, who was part of the Babar murder investigation team, was also killed in a move that Tanoli told reporters was intended to pressure him. This onslaught of murders took place within four months of Babar's murder. A year and a half later, as a trial got under way, Haider was assassinated.

More recently, on September 26, 2013, Naimat Ali Randhawa, a prominent lawyer engaged to be legal counsel for the Babar case, was murdered. Randhawa worked on many high-profile cases and led the Pakistan Muslim League-Nawaz but, according to news reports, the suspect in custody works for the MQM and the police believe the lawyer's pursuit of justice for Babar was the motivation behind the killing.

Rubin's report also looks at threats against two prosecutors working on the case, Muhammad Khan Buriro and Mobashir Mirza. Both men were fired and then fled the country. They told Rubin they had been warned by clerks in their own office who were working as informants for the MQM. According to Buriro, the clerks told him and Mirza that all documents were sent to MQM headquarters. "If you want to see your families," the two were warned, "don't touch this case."

After Haider's murder, Abdul Maroof, the new prosecutor, raised concerns about security. "This is how strong their network is. They located him and killed him just two days before he was supposed to appear in the court," Maroof told the media in Pakistan. "It is negligence on the part of the police for not protecting him." After the Randhawa murder, news reports said Maroof expressed concerns to the court for his own safety should he continue to pursue the Babar case.

When Rubin was asked for this essay about reactions to the killing of Haider and other witnesses among journalists and people she had interviewed, she said: "No one was too surprised. You don't mess with the MQM."

Things are not so different in the Philippines. The Ampatuan family, often described as warlords, similarly dominate their province of Maguindanao, through political office and their private militia. Human rights groups have pointed to the administration of former President Gloria Macapagal Arroyo as having greatly facilitated the rise of Ampatuan power in exchange for political support.

While senior members of the family, including Andal Ampatuan Jr., formerly a local mayor, and Zaldy Ampatuan, the former governor of the Autonomous Region in Muslim Mindanao, are in jail awaiting trial in the massacre—in total eight Ampatuans have been named as primary suspects— many still fear their reach. Over the course of the trial, in addition to the killings of witnesses and others involved in the case, victims' family members—essential to the pursuit of justice in the criminal case and civil complaints—say they have been approached with bribes and threats. Extensive Ampatuan resources have mobilized a defense that has brought year after year of legal stalling tactics, leaving witnesses and complainants vulnerable and under prolonged psychological and financial strain.

"Many members of their clan continue to hold government positions. We, the families of the victims, are nobodies against the powerful Ampatuans," family member Mary Grace Morales said in a 2012 speech to the Foreign Correspondents' Club of Thailand on the anniversary of the massacre.

Combine these coercion tactics with a protection program lacking in funds, capacity, and accountability, and the job of witness can be a hard one to fill. In a 2009 CPJ report, Shawn Crispin looked closely at the decimated life of a witness in the Philippines. Bob Flores was walking with his friend and colleague Dennis Cuesta when assailants fatally shot Cuesta, a radio program director and anchor. Flores, determined to see justice, identified those he saw shoot Cuesta, including a local police officer, to prosecutors, Crispin reported. Then, Flores left his job and uprooted his wife and children, to live on a meager stipend that did not cover his family's basic expenses. Cuesta's suspected killer has not been tried and, by late 2013, Flores remained in the witness protection program.

Victims and advocates also worry that important witnesses are prematurely removed or not accepted into the program. In January 2013, Dennis Aranas, an accomplice-turned-witness in the 2011 murder of Gerardo Ortega, a popular radio host in Puerto Princesa City known for exposing corruption, was found dead in his jail cell. Though Aranas' death was initially labeled a suicide by hanging, a second autopsy at the behest of the family suggested he had first been strangled. Shortly before his death, Aranas was removed from witness protection, ostensibly due to a legal technicality.

"It is alarming because Aranas was under the witness protection program. Then he was taken out of protection. We found him dead," Michaella Ortega, Gerardo Ortega's daughter and spokeswoman for the family, told CPJ at the time. "It affects the morale of the other witnesses by showcasing how inept the government is in ensuring the safety of witnesses." No further steps have been taken to investigate Aranas' death, according to the Ortega family. A gunman in Ortega's murder was convicted in May 2013, but two men believed to have ordered the killing are at large.

These challenges are amplified in the Ampatuan case. Attorney Quinsayas, who has also received threats multiple times over the past few years, pointed out that the sheer number of individuals charged tests the capacity of the witness protection program. "It would be humanly impossible for a few eyewitnesses to identify the almost 200 accused and account for their actions that contributed to the accomplishment of the crime," she told CPJ.

Quinsayas said that a "perennial lack of funds" has plagued the program and that she is concerned that the 25 million Philippine pesos (US$580,000) the government initially budgeted for witness costs for the case are nearly used up. In response to inquiries by family members and their advocates into how witness protection funds have been spent on the trial so far, Department of Justice officials said spending is confidential.

Tight resources have led to much wrangling between the private prosecutors and the Department of Justice over priorities. In response to Quinsayas' request for a security detail to accompany one witness making an affidavit before a public prosecutor, she was told to simply accompany the witness herself. In the end, she had to personally appeal to locally based soldiers to escort them. "The Witness Protection Program of the DOJ is more focused on protecting the program rather than the witnesses," she said.

If there is any upside to the many injustices in the Ampatuan massacre and the Babar murder, it is that these two cases have put a magnifying glass on the issue of killers who murder journalists with impunity in the Philippines and Pakistan and worldwide. In early 2013, the United Nations began to implement an interagency Plan of Action for the Safety of Journalists and Issue of Impunity. The plan, drafted by UNESCO, calls on states to take steps to improve investigations and prosecutions in cases of journalist murders, and, among other measures, improve journalist safety. The plan is global, but it names four countries as initial areas of focus, one of which is Pakistan. The others are Nepal, Iraq, and South Sudan.

Some of this attention may set change in motion and revive the Babar case as well as those of the murdered witnesses. In September 2013, Pakistan's Chief Justice Iftikhar Mohammad Chaudhry took Karachi law enforcement agencies to task. Chaudhry asked for a report on the authorities' failures in the Babar case, including an explanation as to why the witnesses were not provided security despite the Sindh court orders. He also demanded that the killers of the witnesses be arrested. Around the same time, the Sindh provincial assembly passed a witness protection bill to set up a formal witness protection program.

"Wali Khan Babar's murder has at least awakened a Pakistani provincial Assembly in Sindh province to pass a witness protection bill," said journalist Mazhar Abbas of Express News TV. He called it "a ray of hope for those witnesses who are not ready yet to stand up and testify in the murder cases of other journalists killed in Pakistan." It is a hope shared by many in Pakistan, the Philippines, and elsewhere, who want to witness justice, rather than its derailment.

*Elisabeth Witchel, a CPJ consultant, served for many years as the organization's journalist assistance coordinator. She also launched CPJ's Global Campaign against Impunity.*

# One Province Illustrates Colombia's Struggle With Impunity

## By John Otis

**Gen. Rodolfo Palomino, Colombian police chief, writes a message for a campaign supporting FARC demobilization in Tame, Arauca province, on September 18, 2013.**

*Source:* Reuters/Jose Miguel Gomez.

I t took just 24 hours to arrest the gunmen who murdered Henry Rojas Monje, a journalist based in Arauca, a province of Colombia torn by guerrilla war. But for the Rojas family, the pursuit of justice lasted two full decades—and ended in frustration.

A correspondent for *El Tiempo*, Colombia's leading national daily, Rojas often focused on government corruption and ties between Arauca politicians and Marxist rebel groups. On December 28, 1991, Rojas was shot multiple times while in his car. He bled to death on the lap of his 6-year-old son Henry, who was in the passenger seat.

The next day, the police arrested two soldiers, who confessed and were convicted. But the man accused of ordering the Rojas murder, José Gregorio González, the former mayor of the town of Arauca who had been the target of some of the reporter's stories, was eventually cleared and released from prison. By 2011, when the 20-year statute of limitations on murder cases expired, there was still no clarity over who was behind the crime.

"We were very sad when the case was closed," Henry Rojas, the journalist's son, who is now an Arauca lawyer, told CPJ. "The slowness of the legal system breeds impunity."

The legal netherworld of the Rojas case is not some egregious exception: The vast majority of murders of journalists in Colombia have gone unsolved and unpunished. True, the security situation in Colombia over the past decade has improved, which has led to a corresponding reduction in the number of journalist murders. Yet these improvements have outpaced any gains by prosecutors in closing cases and are of no comfort to the families of the many victims of past killings—especially as more cases expire under the 20-year statute of limitations.

Occasionally, the killers are caught and convicted, but the masterminds who target reporters nearly always remain free, CPJ research shows. Problems such as overburdened prosecutors, a lack of information sharing, mishandling of evidence, and malfeasance by judicial officials can delay criminal investigations for years. This favors the perpetrators because as the clock ticks, memories fade, evidence deteriorates, and securing convictions becomes even harder.

Since 1977, the Bogotá-based Foundation for Press Freedom (FLIP) has registered 140 killings of journalists that were job-related.

Of this total, 62 cases, or 44 percent, have been closed because the statute of limitations has run out. The attorney general's office could provide no information on 49 cases because the files had apparently been lost or misplaced. All told, there have been just 19 convictions.

CPJ, which began tracking killings of journalists in 1992 and uses different methodology, has documented 45 journalists and media workers killed directly for their work in Colombia, and an additional 33 killings in which the motive is not clear. In murder cases, impunity reigns in 88 percent, with most of the rest having achieved only partial justice.

As a result, CPJ's 2013 Impunity Index shows little change for Colombia, listing it as the fifth-worst nation for deadly, unpunished violence against the news media, behind only Iraq, Somalia, the Philippines, and Sri Lanka. Colombia has ranked fifth for the past five years on the Index, which calculates the number of unsolved journalist murders as a percentage of each country's population.

This lack of justice is by no means limited to crimes against Colombian journalists. In 2011, *El Tiempo* reported that 90 percent of all people arrested in Bogotá avoided prison sentences due to a judicial system riddled with procedural errors. A recent U.S. State Department report declared that the most serious human rights problems in Colombia are impunity and an overburdened, inefficient justice system that is hindered by subornation and intimidation of judges, prosecutors, and witnesses.

Such threats and coercion are rife in far-flung Colombian provinces where regional authorities rarely manage to solve journalist murders, according to Pedro Vaca, executive director of FLIP. To overcome such obstacles, most cases since 2000 have been shifted to special units within the federal attorney general's office in Bogotá. But changes in jurisdiction, as well as the introduction of a new penal code in 2008, have opened the door to even more procedural delays, confusion, and corruption.

A dismal example is the Henry Rojas case, which was transferred to judicial authorities in Bogotá. Part of the legal process involved his family's quest for government reparations. Though ultimately successful, the effort turned into a 16-year nightmare because Bogotá court officials somehow "lost" the Rojas case file, a mammoth set of documents that stood three feet high and weighed more than 100 pounds.

"Case files don't just get up and walk out the door by themselves," Alejandro Ramelli, a prosecutor for the attorney general's office in Bogotá and an expert on crimes against reporters, told CPJ.

Ramelli blamed two factors for widespread impunity: structural problems within the judicial system, and a single-minded focus by prosecutors on the last link in the chain—those directly responsible for killing journalists—rather than the criminal organizations and corrupt politicians who are often behind the murders.

There have been a few notable breakthroughs.

In 2009, a court in the northern province of Santander sentenced former Barrancabermeja Mayor Julio César Ardila Torres to nearly 29 years in prison on charges of aggravated murder and conspiracy in the 2003 shooting death of local radio reporter José Emeterio Rivas, who had accused Ardila of corruption and ties to paramilitary death squads.

In 2011, the authorities arrested former provincial legislator Ferney Tapasco González, one of the suspected masterminds of the 2002 killing of Orlando Sierra, the deputy editor and muckraking columnist for the Manizales daily newspaper *La Patria*. Sierra had been investigating possible links between Tapasco González and a gang of assassins. The former politician has denied involvement in the killing, and as of this writing the case was still pending.

But such hard-fought advances are rare, and even victories have often turned out to be partial or been reversed on appeal.

"There are so many problems with the legal system in Colombia that people have come to accept the bare minimum," Vaca told CPJ. "That means if there is a conviction, any kind of conviction, we are willing to think that justice has been served. But we must demand full justice."

■ ■ ■

Getting to the bottom of journalist murders is challenging throughout Latin America, but the task can be especially difficult in Colombia, the only country in the hemisphere with an active guerrilla war. The fighting, which began in the 1960s, pits two Marxist rebel groups against the government. Until recently, the mix also included right-wing paramilitary death squads that often collaborated with the national army to fight the guerrillas and with corrupt politicians to intimidate their rivals.

All of these players have been active in Arauca, a sparsely populated but oil-rich province on the Venezuelan border, where six journalists have been killed since 1991, according to FLIP. But no matter the culprit, the Colombian legal system has thus far failed to convict any of the masterminds behind the six murders. Some of the killings may not have been related to the victims' work as journalists, but the inability to solve these crimes feeds the atmosphere of hostility and intimidation for reporters in Arauca.

Take the case of Danilo Alfonso Baquero, a reporter for the now-defunct Emisora Bolivariana radio station in Tame, a town in southwest Arauca province. On Dec. 26, 1993, he was shot dead by men suspected of being guerrillas of the National Liberation Army, known as the ELN, the smaller of Colombia's two rebel insurgencies.

Besides the Baquero murder, the ELN also took responsibility for the 1995 murder of Iván Dario Pelayo, a radio reporter in the town of Puerto Rendón, and the 1996 killing of Alfredo Matiz. A lawyer, politician, and founder in 1965 of Arauca's first radio station, La Voz del Cinaruco, Matiz often used the station to denounce rebel violence, according to his son, Alfredo Matiz Brando.

Relatives have never been able to confirm why the ELN sentenced Baquero, Pelayo, and Matiz to death, nor have they been able to testify at a trial. Arauca province remains an ELN stronghold, and the authorities have been unable or unwilling to arrest the guerrillas who killed the three men or the rebel commanders who presumably ordered the executions. The statute of limitations on the Baquero case expired in December 2013, while it is due to lapse in 2015 in the Pelayo case and in 2016 in the Matiz case.

"Justice is now in the hands of God," Claudia Baquero, the slain journalist's sister, said.

If not justice, some sort of reckoning for these crimes may still be possible. The Colombian government is currently engaged in peace talks in Cuba with the Revolutionary Armed Forces of Colombia, or FARC, the larger of the country's two rebel groups. In July 2013, the FARC asked the government to broaden the peace process to include the ELN, an idea that President Juan Manuel Santos appears to support.

Should a final peace accord with the FARC and ELN emerge, it would likely include a process of transitional justice, which refers to judicial and alternative measures to redress widespread human rights abuses in societies transitioning from war to peace. In the broader interest of persuading the rebels to demobilize, the vast majority of their crimes would go unpunished. However, such a framework could allow for the prosecution of military commanders on all sides who were most responsible for the most serious crimes during the conflict, according to the International Crisis Group.

It's unclear whether such a process would include prosecutions for some of the killings of Colombian journalists. However, both the FARC, whose fighters have also gunned down numerous reporters, and the ELN have endorsed the idea of an independent truth commission to establish the responsibility for crimes and provide reparations.

"Without a doubt, there has also been cruelty and pain provoked by our forces," FARC negotiator Pablo Catatumbo stated in September 2013 on the sidelines of the peace talks in Havana. "We must recognize the need to approach the issue of victims, their identification and reparations with complete loyalty to the cause of peace and reconciliation."

■ ■ ■

For the families of two other murdered Arauca journalists, transitional justice has helped shed some light on the crimes, but it has also proved to be a slow, frustrating, and perplexing legal maze.

On March 18, 2003, Luis Eduardo Alfonso Parada, a correspondent for *El Tiempo* and for the Arauca radio station Meridiano-70, was gunned down by paramilitaries on his way to work. His death came just nine months after paramilitaries killed the station's owner, Efraín Varela Noriega, who, like Alfonso, was an outspoken critic of the death squads that had recently deployed in Arauca.

Several paramilitary fighters involved in the two murders turned themselves in under Colombia's 2005 Justice and Peace law. This transitional justice legal mechanism, which over the past decade has helped bring about the demobilization of about 30,000 paramilitary members, offers reduced sentences—with a maximum of eight years in prison— to former fighters who tell the truth about their crimes and agree to provide reparations.

Under the law, a former paramilitary fighter confessed in 2009 to killing Alfonso. But the Alfonso family lawyer, Ramón del Carmen Garcés, told CPJ that the man has yet to be convicted in the murder due to procedural delays.

More allegations about the Alfonso and Varela killings emerged from Miguel Ángel Mejía, who commanded paramilitary forces in Arauca in the early 2000s. In testimony in 2009 under the Justice and Peace law, Mejía accused former Arauca Gov. Julio Acosta Bernal of receiving financial backing from the paramilitaries and of ordering the militiamen to kill the two journalists. Acosta has since been arrested and imprisoned on charges of murdering a rival Arauca politician. But no charges have been filed against him in the deaths of Alfonso and Varela, who often criticized Acosta in their reports. The former governor has denied any involvement.

In any case, eight years after the Justice and Peace law went into effect, it has led to just 14 convictions of paramilitary fighters. In a 2013 report, Amnesty International called the law "another example of how the state fails to meet international standards on the right of victims to truth, justice, and reparation."

Efforts by CPJ to interview government prosecutors handling the Alfonso and Varela cases were unsuccessful.

"To achieve justice, we have to get the person who gave the orders," Garcés told CPJ from his law office in Arauca. "That person is much more of a criminal than the one who pulled the trigger."

Garcés points out that even though it's been more than a decade since a reporter was killed in the province, local journalism has never recovered. Those who dig too deeply into government corruption, ties between politicians and criminals, or guerrilla actions, are quickly warned off.

"These are untouchable issues," said one Arauca reporter who was assigned a government escort last year after receiving numerous death threats. "The objective of the killers to silence the press in any way possible was achieved. Those of us who survived received a very strong message."

*John Otis*, *CPJ's Andes correspondent for the Americas program, works as a correspondent for* Time *magazine and the* Global Post. *He is the author of the 2010 book* Law of the Jungle, *about U.S. military contractors kidnapped by Colombian rebels, and is based in Bogotá, Colombia.*

# 8

CENSORED

# Gunmen Rule Neza and the Press on Outskirts of Mexico City

*By Mike O'Connor*

**Police officers stand guard near a crime scene in Neza, on the outskirts of Mexico City, on January 16, 2011.**

*Source:* Reuters/Jorge Dan.

If you're coming into Mexico City's airport, just before you touch down, you're really flying over the large city called Neza. As your plane taxis, on the left, for miles, that's Neza. Though it's not in what is called the Federal District, the legal term for Mexico's capital, Neza is part of the metropolis that we think of as Mexico City.

"There are usually four of them in the car," a police officer in Neza said. "They drive up close to you and show their assault rifles. They say, 'This territory is ours. Get out.' You turn around. There is no clearer way to know they have taken over the city."

There are three important points here.

One, Neza, about 10 miles southeast of the center of Mexico City, which has a little over 1 million people, is part of metropolitan Mexico City, where the politicians keep saying there are no organized crime cartels. Miguel Ángel Mancera, Mexico City's mayor, forcefully told an interviewer that in his city, "There is not a single cartel. Nothing like the names of cartels you find in the states."

Two, the men who told the police officer they have taken over are cartel hit men.

Finally, the press in Neza, local reporters and those who write for national papers, do not cover stories like that because, they say, they are under threat. So the public does not know that the police say hit men run the streets here.

Another officer in Neza said, "If you see a big SUV, you just turn around and don't go down the street. It's their street. Or the same for a car with blacked out windows and no license plates." A third officer told CPJ, "They got me again about 10 days ago and I'm ashamed. They made me leave the area. I'm ashamed because they can make me run away in my own city."

People call this place Neza because its real name is long and complicated. It was named after Nezahualcóyotl, a pre-Columbian leader. You cannot tell where the capital of the country stops and Neza starts. One is on one side of a street with four stray dogs, and the other is 20 feet of concrete away at a stack of broken and scattered plastic beer cases. Don't ask which side is Neza, which side is technically Mexico City, because it doesn't matter.

A mid-level police officer said that about four years ago Neza's leaders simply "turned over" the city to the Familia Michoacana, one of the country's top cartels, to let it run wild with drug sales, kidnapping, and wholesale extortion of businesses. Interestingly, that's the same way journalists describe it. They use the same term "turned over," or sometimes "handed over," or maybe "sold." The journalists say they can't write about that because they would be killed.

"The other reporters and I saw what was happening in other states, like in the north, where the cartels were setting businesses on fire if they didn't pay extortion. But we thought it could never reach the capital," said a reporter for a national newspaper. "And we never thought we'd be threatened here. We were wrong about both of those things. They are burning businesses, they have taken over, and we are getting threats."

Over more than three months, CPJ conducted extensive and repeated interviews with 12 reporters and photographers in Nezahualcóyotl as well as interviews with nine police officers and more than 30 people who run small and medium-size businesses in Neza and in small towns nearby, from a flower shop owner early in the morning to strip bar owners late at night.

Everyone was granted anonymity in exchange for frank interviews. The identities of most people interviewed were kept secret from most of the others interviewed. Protecting the identity of sources was paramount in reseaching this report because of the thick atmosphere of danger in the city. There was remarkable consistency in what people had to say within each group. The focus of the research was on the journalists and on the information they are afraid to share with the public.

■ ■ ■

A new mayor, Juan Zepeda, took office in January 2013. He said the town had been given over to the cartel, though he's hoping to correct that. "Once they're in here I wonder if we can get them out. We're doing better, I think, but my police are infiltrated. The state and the federal police are infiltrated by the cartel. You have police committing crimes on their own or for the cartel."

The mayor said he cannot protect the ordinary citizen if he reports a crime to the police because they may well inform the cartel and the cartel will take revenge on the citizen. "If I can't protect a person who reports one crime how am I going to protect reporters who cover what the cartel does all the time?" he said. "I can't, and reporters can't cover what the cartel is doing."

Mireya Cuellar, the national editor of *La Jornada* newspaper, said it has been extraordinarily frustrating to see the cartels march through much of Mexico and not be able to report it. "They aren't knocking on the door of the capital any longer," she said. "They are in the kitchen now, and we can't tell anyone they're here." *La Jornada* no longer reports on organized crime in Neza. "The tragedy is that you can't say what you know is happening. Just like you can't say in so many of the states," Cuellar said. "Your correspondent may be at least abducted or beaten or even killed. Apparently there is no government that can protect you."

"The tendency in Neza," said Carlos Benavides, assistant managing editor of the national newspaper *El Universal*, "is the same as in the states where cartels have taken power. Reporters have to step back and not do what we all would like them to be able to do."

To stay alive in Neza journalists simply stop telling the public what the cartel doesn't want the public to know. All of the journalists CPJ spoke with who cover Neza said they stay away from organized crime stories or play it very cautiously. For the most part, they don't investigate or look for the big picture. They crank out today's limited story and hope the cartel doesn't get angry.

Since the cartel came in, according to police officers and reporters, crime has spiked in every category. But not officially. As the mayor said, people run a big risk if they report a crime. A lot of the crimes that are not reported but are often discussed are common burglaries and robberies and the like, which reporters said are below the level of the cartel.

While admitting that a great percentage of crimes go unreported, city officials would not make public details on crimes citizens do report. The city's chief spokesman, Roberto Perez, repeatedly told CPJ that the mayor and the police chief were working to release crime statistics for the past several years, but after 12 days, and as the deadline for this report passed, all that was released were auto theft figures. Perez could not explain why the city had not released the other information. The car theft data showed a spike of more than 400 percent between 2006 and 2012, putting Neza in third place nationally for that crime, according to the city. Interestingly, the numbers come from car insurance companies, not the victims themselves. We don't know how many uninsured citizens were brave enough to report a theft.

If you're afraid to report that you were held up on the bus by a drug addict—an increasing problem, reporters say—you're really not going to tell police your business is being extorted every month by the cartel. The reporters who spoke to CPJ estimate that perhaps 60 percent of Neza's businesses are forced to pay the cartel. The mid-level police officer, who also has a city-wide view, thought it was probably under 50 percent of the businesses. But when you're in the approximate area of half of all the businesses, a difference of several percentage points is not worth quibbling about.

In early 2009, the leader of the association of 300 stall owners at one of the markets in town received a phone call from a man who said he represented the Familia Michoacana. The caller had a deal to offer. He gave the association leader a very good description of details of his closest family members and their habits as well as those of other association leaders, according to one of the six members of the association's board of directors.

The deal was simple: Call the board together, and then the stall owners, and tell them that from now on every owner pays the equivalent of about US$60 to begin with and then about US$8 a month. That way, no one would be killed. Each member now drops off the money in an envelope at the association office on a day announced monthly, and someone picks it up.

Actually, people connected to the market have been killed since that call, according to stall owners. But they don't know if it's the common street crime killings that are on the rise anyway, or if the murders are messages from the extortionists.

Market venders estimate there are 70 markets in Neza, each with an average of 300 stalls, and that all except one of the markets pays. No one at that market, the San Juan, wanted to talk about the subject. When you add it all up, it is a lot of money for the cartel.

The payments have gone up by about US$2 a month from a year ago. "I can manage the extortion up to now. That's not the point," a stall owner surrounded by the smells of fresh vegetables told CPJ. "First, this money is only the beginning. Of course they will squeeze us. They're killers and criminals. They will squeeze us tomorrow. And second, we have no protection from the authorities because the police are afraid or they are part of it."

The member of the association's board of directors said that already owners of ordinary stores in the city, not market stalls, were being hit with much higher—often unpayable—extortion demands and were closing.

The publisher of a local paper who said he had written in a column that city police officers sometimes collected extortion money, apparently for the cartel, said he received a death threat. Now, he stays away from news like that, he said. Reporters for national papers didn't touch that story either.

It's not fair to say there have been no news stories about some of the problems in Neza. For instance, the giant national newspaper *El Universal* ran an interesting article in June 2012 that covered the cartel, drug sales and extortion and even touched on corruption in the local police. In May 2012, the national paper *Reforma* had two mid-length stories on extortion, then let the matter drop. But no story went nearly as deeply as the problems seem to go. None mentioned the police or press being too scared to do their jobs, for instance. In addition, they were one-shot efforts. As reporters grow more fearful, coverage since, by any newspaper, has not given readers anything like the whole picture.

This happened in a town near Neza. The name of the town will have to be a secret to protect the identity of the people who shared the details, but those details are important because they are how terror and the control spreads. Two teenagers rolled up on a motorbike with a note and gave it to the dispatcher of a bus cooperative. Each cooperative member owns a small bus or maybe a couple. Each member is also a driver. The note said that some men wanted to meet the president of the co-op. The dispatcher took it as a joke: After all, who listens to two kids on a motorbike?

Then came the phoned threats, with details about people's families, and there was a meeting with demands that for each bus the men wanted 50 pesos a week. Not so much, about US$4. That would be a start. The bus drivers checked around the whole area and found that all the other bus co-ops were paying extortion. Still, they said, no. So, two drivers were murdered and one was kidnapped. He was released after the rest agreed to the weekly extortion. One lesson hidden behind this is that even in the small community of cooperative bus drivers the fear of the cartel is so great it was not known that wholesale extortion was occurring.

The two murders were covered as news stories by local papers. But just as murders. There was nothing in the stories to connect the deaths to extortion. In fact, the stories were played as armed robberies gone wrong. There was nothing about the abduction. There was nothing to tell the public that a cartel was extorting all the bus companies in the whole area. And, by extension, the authorities were powerless, afraid, or corrupt.

It's not only the cartel that keeps crime stories down, reporters say, there's a city police policy to keep crime out of the press because it makes them look incompetent or corrupt. With cartel lookouts now lurking at the locations of cartel murders, reporters and photographers usually don't go there in person anymore, they say. They try to cover the story by telephone. But that's when, they say, they can run into a news blackout.

A reporter described it this way: "We get a call from citizens that there's been a murder on let's say street corner X. If we call the police, they say there's nothing. The ambulance service says there's nothing. The citizens are watching the police at the scene examining the body or they see the body go into the coroner's vehicle. The coroner says they have no information. So, there is no story. There was no murder at street corner X."

■ ■ ■

Neza was a problem for Mexico City for centuries. It was a lake until the early 20th century, Lake Texcoco, but that flooded a lot, even under the Aztecs, so it was gradually drained. Most of the land went to extremely poor migrants from the rest of the country who became Mexico City's worst-paid workers. Some of the land became the city's vast garbage dump, though that's almost all landfill now.

In the late 1990s a homegrown cartel took over, according to Neza police officers and Zepeda, Neza's mayor, who was a city official then. But only in a limited way. Just marijuana and cocaine sales. Still, even that made it very unusual for Mexico, because relatively few Mexicans used drugs of any kind in those days. Drugs went north, to Americans.

The gang had a complete lock on drug sales in Neza, and it controlled the city, state, and federal police, when it came to its business, so in that way it was similar to the cartel that controls the city today, say old-time journalists and Rafael Macedo de la Concha, the federal attorney general at the time. The cartel also had a middle-aged woman in charge with the romantic name of Ma Baker. That's right, in English, Ma Baker. No one knows why. Or rather, everyone who was active then has different explanations for why. Her real name was Delia Buendía Gutiérrez.

Ma Baker's cartel ran perhaps 400 retail outlets in Neza's 25 square miles, tightly squashed together with misery and customers. The city is one of the most densely populated in Mexico. Her cartel did well enough that in 2002, Rafael Macedo, the federal attorney general, said in a speech in Mexico City at the National Anthropological Museum that she was staying out of jail by paying off public officials, including judges.

Then, somehow, things went crazy. In seven months in 2002, two senior federal prosecutors and two senior federal police officers, all working on Neza narcotics investigations, were assassinated. The federal investigations led to Ma Baker and her gang. The federal attorney general's office went after her, and soon she and those at the very top of the cartel were in jail, except for a few who were fugitives.

The cartel was broken. But not the vast number of people who ran it, or were corrupted by it, or who murdered police officers and competitors for it. According to newspapers archives, there were only moderate sentences for a few. The police chief of Neza did get a 25-year sentence, but almost the entire city government and police force were either on the cartel's payroll or at least looking the other way. The same for a number of state police and federal authorities, according to journalists and federal investigators from those days. Both the journalists and the investigators asked not to be named, out of fear.

■ ■ ■

For several years, reporters say, no one owned the drug game in Neza. There were lots of drugs, but there wasn't a dominant cartel. Then a new group came in shooting. The murders picked up in 2008 or 2009, according to reporters. First, the cartel took over the drug sales as a monopoly, like Ma Baker. But then, crucially, it began to make the change to what we have now, the new Mexican way of cartels, the way they work in the rest of the country, a fight for territory. In Neza, too, where retail drug sales are important, but only part of the business, the cartel ballooned to include control of the streets—not always, to be sure, but it seems they have control when they want it. Then, kidnapping, and massive extortion across the city.

An organized crime cartel was never supposed to operate in metropolitan Mexico City. Middle and upper classes in the capital, where political, cultural, and intellectual power is concentrated, tend to look down on the rest of the country. The drug war was supposed to be taking place out there, in the "provinces."

But news coverage of the states where cartels are gaining influence or control has been badly hurt by the same problem that keeps Mexico City uninformed about what's happening in Neza: Reporters in the states often can't report the real story because they are under threat from organized crime. So, few people are aware of the cartels' spread, state by state, let alone that they have reached Mexico City.

To a great extent, the Mexican public thinks that this fight, this "Drug War," is exclusively about drugs, and that the customers are almost exclusively Americans.

The Familia Michoacana sells drugs only to Mexicans in Neza. The rest of its pursuits involve kidnapping and extortion and prostitution, according to reporters who cover the city. The deep problem for Mexican journalism and for Mexicans is that while those reporters can tell CPJ that, they can't tell their readers in the rest of the country. But if they could, then the readers and policy makers might take another look at some of their assumptions about what's called the "Drug War," and what it may take to win it.

*CPJ Mexico Representative* **Mike O'Connor** *is a veteran journalist who has reported for news organizations including* CBS News, National Public Radio, *and* The New York Times. *He is the author of the 2013* Attacks on the Press *essay, "The Zacatecas Rules: Cartel's Reign Cannot Be Covered."*

# A Sliver of Hope Emerges for a More Independent Press in Turkey

*By Nicole Pope*

**A Turkish riot policeman pushes a photographer during a protest at Taksim Square in Istanbul on June 11, 2013. Journalists covering the protests at Gezi Park were often deliberately targeted by police.**

*Source:* Reuters/Murad Sezer.

The protests that erupted in Istanbul's Gezi Park in May 2013 not only introduced a new, restless generation of Turks—urban, educated, middle class, and determined to be heard—but also exposed the inability and unwillingness of Turkey's cowed media to report their demands.

Riot police brutally dislodged a small group of demonstrators who had been staging a peaceful sit-in at the park to oppose plans to build a shopping mall on the last public green space near Taksim Square. The heavy-handed crackdown set off further protests, which spread to other cities.

Viewers who tuned in to their favorite television channels in the first days of the unrest found little or no coverage of the protests, but were offered instead a selection of cooking programs and talk shows. A documentary on penguins was aired on CNN Türk while CNN International was broadcasting scenes of protest from the park to the rest of the world. The penguin documentary seemed so incongruous in the circumstances that the seabird became, and has remained, a symbol of national resistance for the young.

Over the following days and weeks, as demonstrations spread to other cities, Prime Minister Recep Tayyip Erdoğan set the tone for the news media in strident speeches denouncing the protesters as looters and hooligans. He also railed against foreign conspiracies, variously blaming the unrest on "the interest rate lobby" and foreign powers jealous of Turkey's success.

The "deafening silence" of the local media, as Stefan Füle, a European Union commissioner, put it, exposed both direct government pressure and the unwillingness of media proprietors to risk the loss of lucrative public contracts by fulfilling their role as a watchdog of democracy.

The Gezi Park clash has nevertheless had some positive outcomes, including a galvanized youth who might dream of a more democratic future, and it has forced some independent-minded reporters and columnists fired for their work to join new modest but independent news outlets to confront the country's muzzled media head on.

This is not a challenge to be overcome overnight. An independent press needs to find a self-sustaining economic model that does not rely on government largesse, and Turkey's few but vociferous champions of press freedom face a nation deeply divided socially and politically.

■ ■ ■

As the Gezi Park crisis grew, so did the polarization of the society and the news media. A new low was reached when the daily newspaper *Takvim* published a fake interview with Christiane Amanpour under the headline "Dirty confession" in which the celebrated British-Iranian reporter (who is a member of CPJ's board of directors) was falsely quoted as saying she had been paid to destabilize Turkey.

In the absence of unfettered coverage, Turks turned to social media, where they could find a broad variety of views, to fill the gap. They did so in such large numbers that Erdoğan described Twitter and other social media as "the worst menace to society." Many viewers also turned to Halk TV, a channel close to the main opposition Republican People's Party, which can hardly be described as unbiased. It was broadcasting live footage from Taksim Square and other trouble spots.

For several weeks, riot police clashed with demonstrators, who took to the streets across the country. Altogether, six people died and thousands were injured in the turmoil. Reporters and photographers on the scene were often deliberately targeted as the police used tear gas, water cannons, and rubber bullets to disperse the crowds. The independent Turkish press agency Bianet counted 153 journalists who suffered blows and 39 who were detained between May and September 2013.

Not content with putting pressure on local media, Turkish officials also turned against representatives of the foreign press. Italian journalist Mattia Cacciatori, 24, was charged with "violating the law on public gatherings and demonstrations" and resisting arrest. The case was pending in late 2013. Ankara Mayor Melih Gökcek took to Twitter to accuse BBC correspondent Selin Girit of being a "foreign agent."

"A cabinet minister openly accused me on Twitter of spreading lies and false propaganda against the government," said Amberin Zaman, Turkey correspondent for *The Economist* and a columnist for the daily newspaper *Taraf*. Zaman and other journalists posting regular updates and denouncing police violence on social media became the targets of particularly vicious campaigns organized by anonymous trolls defending the government and threatening the reporters with death and sexual assault.

Turkey gradually returned to an uneasy calm, which has been interrupted from time to time by sporadic flare-ups. But the Gezi events have made a lasting impression on Turkish society, even though the clampdown on the media continues. The Turkish Union of Journalists announced in July that 22 journalists had been dismissed and 37 forced to quit because of the positions they adopted during the unrest. Yavuz Baydar, former ombudsman for *Sabah* newspaper, lost his position when he criticized his newspaper's coverage of the Gezi events and denounced the media's craven self-censorship in a *New York Times* op-ed on July 19. Can Dündar, another well-known commentator, was laid off by *Milliyet* on August 1.

Pressure on the media has been building for several years. In 2013, Turkey was the top jailer of journalists, ahead of Iran and China, according to CPJ's annual prison census. At least 40 journalists, many of them Kurds, were being held because of their work. "Government pressure is the most urgent issue," said Ceren Sözeri, who teaches in the Mass Media and Communications department at Galatasaray University.

A country in transition, Turkey has undergone a major economic and social transformation in the past decade. In spite of reforms, it still suffers a democratic deficit. The Justice and Development Party, which came to power in 2002, has now asserted its authority over the army, which was the dominant force in the country for decades. In the absence of strong opposition parties promoting democratic rights, this success has led to an excessive concentration of power in the hands of the ruling party. After he won a third term in office in June 2011, Erdoğan gave free rein to his authoritarian and intolerant tendencies.

Turkey's penal code and its Anti-Terror Law, which protects ideological boundaries defined by the state, are still used to silence journalists, mainly those of Kurdish origin, but state oppression is not the only obstacle to press freedom in Turkey. "The ownership structure is another issue, as is the fact that owners and editors often share the state's ideological views," said Sözeri, who cowrote a comprehensive report on the political economy of Turkey's media sector, published by the think tank TESEV in 2011. That same year, Erdoğan summoned the editors of major media outlets to dictate the acceptable limits of their coverage of the Kurdish conflict. Many complied with his demands.

Historically, strong ties have always existed between the state and the media in Turkey. In the early days of the Republic and even in late Ottoman times, newspapers were seen as instruments of the state's civilizing mission. As a result, prominent journalists have often crossed into the political arena, becoming members of Parliament or government officials. In July 2013, following this tradition, Erdoğan picked Yiğit Bulut, a former *Habertürk* columnist and television presenter, to be his chief adviser. Bulut is known mainly for suggesting that foreign powers were attempting to kill Erdoğan from afar using telekinesis. Other government officials continue to publish newspaper columns.

The unholy alliance that exists between media proprietors and officialdom is based largely on business interests. It undermines Turkey's democracy by preventing the media from playing its role as a watchdog. In the past few years, the media landscape has been transformed as government cronies acquired newspapers and television channels, in some cases by securing loans from public banks, tightening the ruling party's hold on the sector. But even groups that aren't owned by government supporters have to take political sensitivities into consideration. In 2009, the Doğan group was slapped with a record US$2.5 billion tax fine, which forced it to sell two daily newspapers, *Milliyet* and *Vatan*. The fine was widely viewed as a politically motivated step to restrain the company, whose flagship newspaper *Hürriyet* was critical of the government.

With few exceptions, mainstream newspapers and television stations are loss-making enterprises, but they open the gate to lucrative public tenders and state contracts. Journalists perceived to put these deals at risk are pre-emptively dismissed. "I was warned twice," said Zaman, who wrote a column twice weekly in *Habertürk* until she was laid off in April when she failed to tone down her articles.

"Every media owner owns at least one hydroelectric plant," said Sözeri, the co-author of the report on Turkey's media. "All media groups have participated in public tenders and won construction or

mining contracts." In 1994, a ban was imposed preventing media owners from participating in public tenders, but it was lifted less than a
decade later, after intense lobbying by media groups. A degree of loyalty is also ensured through the distribution of advertising by state-
owned companies.

■ ■ ■

Caught between direct political pressure and an implicit code of conduct expected of media owners, journalists are vulnerable. Fears of
unemployment and political polarization have so far prevented them
from fighting back through collective action. "There is no sense of solidarity in the sector, because journalists have too much to lose," said
Aslı Tunç, head of the Media School at Istanbul Bilgi University. "The
sector didn't invest in good reporting, but in opinion making." A class
system rules whereby reporters, the fact finders, are often poorly remu-
nerated, while big-name columnists command extravagant salaries.
"The perks offered to some Turkish columnists are, I think, unparal-
leled, and the frequency to which they are permitted to write gives
them great power," Zaman said.

To secure their well-paid positions, those in management positions
need to be finely attuned to what is at stake for the proprietors. "If you
become editor-in-chief, understanding the owner's behavior, knowing his
investment portfolio and his expectations from the government, is more
important than having qualifications in the media industry," Sözeri said.

The Gezi debacle unveiled to the public the multifaceted challenges that journalists face in their work and the lack of a culture of
independent journalism. "One of the few positive aspects of Gezi
and the media is that the ownership structure has begun to be discussed. People became aware of the situation," said Tunç. "For the first
time, media employees have also reacted. For instance at NTV, camera people left their posts in protest. They went outside and joined the
demonstrators."

The failure of news outlets at Gezi Park has led to new quests
and turned the focus on smaller outlets that attach more value to
strong editorial content. "There was a strong reaction because for the
first time, problems were exposed with such nakedness," said Doğan

Akın, editor-in-chief of T24, an online news website founded in 2009 to provide independent news coverage. "For us, it's an opportunity. During the Gezi events, our figures quadrupled. Now we have 80,000 to 120,000 daily visitors."

Operating on a shoe-string budget, T24 is training young reporters to produce solid news stories. The seasoned journalists who write opinion pieces on the site are, for the most part, not paid for their contributions. "We need inspiration," said Tunç. "We are so fed up with crooks and bad intentions. Such platforms should increase in numbers." But while these alternative news sources are growing in popularity, they have yet to develop a viable business model that will allow them to offer decent pay to their employees.

T24 launched a readers fund to support its expansion and raised more than 100,000 Turkish lira (about US$50,000) through crowd funding in October 2013—a first in Turkey. Akın and a few prominent journalists, many of them T24 contributors, recently founded Punto24: Platform for Independent Journalism, an organization that aims to improve ethical and editorial standards. Other founders included Hasan Cemal, a veteran columnist who was fired by *Milliyet* in March 2013, and Yasemin Çongar, former deputy editor of *Taraf* newspaper, which played a pioneering role in independent coverage and lifted the veil of immunity that protected the military.

Few people expect the post–Gezi Park era to produce rapid and significant improvements in the Turkish media, despite its perilous state. "People make romantic assessments, but in fact we still have the same twisted structure. It would be too optimistic to expect things to change drastically and rapidly," Akın warned. "For us, to be truly alternative, we have to improve, to raise our standards. Only then can this new structure challenge the old," he said.

"You can't separate general expectations from the overall culture of democracy or lack thereof in Turkey," said Zaman. "Investigative journalism hasn't been given its due in Turkey, because the media was viewed by owners as a way of expanding their power." The recent unrest has demonstrated that as long as journalists fail to unite, they remain vulnerable to political pressure. Yet the social and political divisions that cut through society are just as deep among members of the media, preventing effective collective action. "Gezi prompted a realignment and hardening of existing positions, leading to a very deep polarization that now continues," Zaman said. With three elections—local, presidential and legislative—scheduled in 2014 and 2015, these divisions are unlikely to be bridged in the short term.

But Gezi has also revealed the coming of a new generation, more open to the world and to cultural diversity. "I'm not too pessimistic because I'm working with young people," said Tunç of Istanbul Bilgi University. "We have to be patient; it will take time. But this old-fashioned mentality cannot go on. Young people are resourceful. They're innovative."

The Gezi generation, Sözeri points out, belongs mainly to the social group that advertisers target: educated, well-to-do consumers who want a comfortable life. "The mainstream media have noticed that they could lose their readers, their audience," she said. "The circulation of newspapers has decreased since Gezi, and television channels were badly affected too."

The ruling Justice and Development Party remains the dominant political force in the country, but the unrest signalled growing resistance to the paternalistic and authoritarian form of governance that has long held sway in Turkey, particularly among young people. In their current state, mainstream media don't meet their expectations. "What Gezi touched off exposed a whole slice of population that we were unaware of. They demonstrated their ability to take a political stand, and they will be expecting more," Zaman said. "It means that the media has to either undergo a total revision of operating philosophy or die."

*Nicole Pope* *is a Swiss journalist based in Istanbul. She was Turkey corre-spondent for the daily* Le Monde *for 15 years and currently works as a colum-nist and independent researcher. She is the author of* Honor Killings in the Twenty-First Century *and co-author of* Turkey Unveiled: A History of Modern Turkey.

# 9

# TRENDS IN PRESS FREEDOM

# CPJ's Risk List: Where Press Freedom Suffered

*By Maya Taal*

Supporters of the Muslim Brotherhood try to push a journalist, center, away from the police academy where ousted President Mohamed Morsi was on trial on the outskirts of Cairo, November 4, 2013. Perhaps nowhere did press freedom decline more dramatically in 2013 than in polarized Egypt.

*Source:* Reuters/Amr Abdallah Dalsh.

On August 31, 2013, *Der Spiegel* reported that the United States' National Security Agency (NSA) had hacked into the private communications of Qatari broadcaster Al-Jazeera. The German news magazine, citing documents leaked by former NSA contractor Edward Snowden, reported that the NSA deemed its operation to access the communications of interesting targets specially protected by Al-Jazeera "a notable success."

As of late in the year, the action against Al-Jazeera was the only reported instance of the NSA directly spying on any news outlet. But continuing revelations based on the documents obtained by Snowden paint a picture of wide-ranging surveillance by the U.S. and its allies—surveillance that presents a clear threat to global Internet privacy and therefore to freedom of the press worldwide. Digital communication has become essential to newsgathering, and the decentralized nature of the Internet has until now sheltered many journalists around the world who are restricted from reporting or expressing their opinion in traditional media. Furthermore, the U.S. government has undermined its own global leadership position on free expression and Internet openness, especially when it comes to battling efforts by repressive countries like China and Iran to restrict the Internet.

"Countries who seek to gain control over their people through the Internet have their own agendas. They are in search of larger governmental control or even censorship online," said Marietje Schaake, a member of the European Parliament and leader on Internet freedom issues. "We must ensure the NSA-triggered debate does not become a race to the bottom," she told CPJ.

The mass surveillance programs by the U.S. and U.K., as well as restrictive Internet legislation by various governments and a wave of cyberattacks globally, are among the alarming developments that have landed cyberspace on CPJ's Risk List.

CPJ developed the Risk List in 2012 to highlight countries where press freedom is on the decline. This year, we chose to add the supranational platform of cyberspace to the list because of the profound erosion of freedom on the Internet, a critical sphere for journalists worldwide. In 2013, CPJ also identified Egypt and Bangladesh, torn apart by political polarization, with journalists caught in the middle; Syria, which continues to be wracked by violent conflict; and authoritarian Vietnam. Also included are Ecuador, Liberia, Russia, Turkey, and Zambia—all nominal democracies where the space for free expression and independent newsgathering is rapidly shrinking.

The list is based on the expertise of CPJ staff, but also takes into account press freedom indicators such as journalist fatalities and imprisonments, restrictive legislation, state censorship, impunity in anti-press attacks, and journalists driven into exile. Those places on the Risk List are not the worst press freedom offenders, but rather spots where CPJ documented the most significant deterioration of the media climate during 2013. Countries on CPJ's first Risk List in 2012 but not on this year's list have not necessarily improved—they have simply been displaced by more recent developments.

Trends witnessed in 2013 include:

- Deterioration in several indicators, including fatalities and censorship, in Egypt
- New legislation to stifle free speech in Ecuador, Liberia, Russia, Vietnam, and Zambia
- Firings and forced resignations of journalists in Turkey at the government's behest
- Targeted violence against journalists in Bangladesh and Russia, and a soaring rate of abductions in Syria
- Crackdowns on online journalism in Russia, Vietnam, and Bangladesh

Perhaps nowhere did press freedom decline more dramatically in 2013 than Egypt, where persecution of critical reporters under President Mohamed Morsi was radically reversed mid-way through the year when the military ousted him from office and launched a crackdown on pro-Morsi news outlets. At least six journalists had been killed as of late in the year, making the country the second deadliest place to work after Syria. Dozens of journalists were detained at least briefly. In addition to state-sponsored censorship, a climate of self-censorship took root.

Negative trends in Liberia and Zambia are of special concern as both are led by governments that promised a new era of freedom of expression. Instead, both places were marked by the continuous and public vilification of the press by authorities, and the systematic muzzling of journalists through the courts. Turkey had already damaged its image as a rising democracy by abusing anti-terror laws to imprison journalists, especially Kurdish ones. Through both verbal and physical attacks on local and international journalists during the Gezi Park protests, Turkey further squeezed the space for independent reporting.

Ecuador and Russia both implemented wide-ranging, vague legislation that gives the government extensive powers to stifle dissent. Ecuador, already known for its abuse of defamation laws, adopted a new Communications Law with broad powers of censorship. The law will be enforced by a state watchdog loyal to President Rafael Correa. Vladimir Putin's return to the presidency was marked by a rollback of the modest reforms under Dmitry Medvedev, and an increasingly hostile atmosphere for the press. Vietnam issued a new decree that greatly restricted speech on the Internet, a move that threatens the bloggers who represent the country's only independent media.

Political polarization wracked Bangladesh in 2013, and the line between politics and journalism became more blurred than ever. Journalists were attacked from all sides during a series of protests sparked by political wounds and religious tensions dating back to the country's secession from Pakistan in 1971.

In Syria, extremely dangerous conditions for reporters became even worse. In addition to remaining the deadliest country for journalists, abductions became increasingly common, making it nearly impossible to cover the uprising.

Here are capsule reports on the 10 places named to the CPJ Risk List:

## Cyberspace

Profound new threats to journalists emerged in the supranational sphere of cyberspace in 2013. The Internet revolutionized the practice of journalism largely by the absence of government control, but its decentralized nature was in jeopardy as many countries stepped up efforts to monitor or disrupt the free flow of digital information.

News stories based on classified documents obtained from former NSA contractor Snowden revealed extensive surveillance both within and without U.S. borders, potentially chilling newsgathering activities, which rely on confidentiality. Experts say the collection of metadata gives authorities the capability to map a journalist's contacts and activity via transactional records such as the time and date of phone calls, the numbers called, location data, and more.

"Everybody is afraid to be a source," said Thomas Peele, a veteran investigative reporter based in the San Francisco Bay area. "Now, reporters are back to looking for payphones, and red flags in flower pots, because anybody knows that to use a government email to contact a reporter on the fly, or to be in a government office, use a government-issued phone or cell phone to contact a reporter, to use a private email account, but logged on through a government computer, can very easily be found out in this day and age."

Journalists and sources outside the U.S. are particularly vulnerable to exposure because they do not enjoy the privacy protections afforded by U.S. law. According to *The Guardian*, the U.K.'s electronic eavesdropping and security agency, GCHQ, cooperates with the NSA to gather information from technology companies. Also in the U.K., a bill labeled the "snooper's charter" by critics, which would give law enforcement greater ability to monitor Internet use, was still being promoted by some British officials in late 2013 despite strong opposition from certain politicians.

Violations of digital privacy by the U.S. and U.K. governments undermine their moral authority and ability to challenge other countries that restrict Internet freedom. These include China, one of the staunchest critics of U.S. Internet hegemony. In September, Chinese authorities squeezed already-tight controls over social media with new rules that could result in prison time for users who post comments deemed libelous that are widely reposted. In Singapore, a new licensing scheme for news websites was seen as a way to extend censorship of traditional media to the Internet. Bahraini authorities hacked into social media accounts to prosecute their anonymous users. These moves were in addition to repressive action against online journalists in Bangladesh, Russia, and Vietnam as detailed elsewhere in the Risk List.

A wave of cyberattacks also hit a range of media outlets in 2013. Both *The New York Times* and *The Wall Street Journal* reported attempts by Chinese hackers to access their communications. Leading up to June elections in Iran, opposition websites were hacked, and Google said tens of thousands of Iranian email users were targeted. The Syrian Electronic Army claimed credit for several cyberattacks, including one on the Twitter feed of the Associated Press, where a false tweet about a White House explosion caused the Dow Jones Industrial Average to fall 143 points. Further from the centers of global power, journalists covering armed conflict in Burma said their email accounts were compromised by state-sponsored attackers. The Guatemalan news outlet *elPeriódico* said it had been targeted in a series of cyberattacks as it published stories alleging corruption in President Otto Pérez Molina's administration.

## Egypt

Over the year, the Egyptian press became increasingly polarized politically. While in power, Mohamed Morsi, of the Muslim Brotherhood, and his allies used highly charged rhetoric and legal harassment to intimidate critical journalists. CPJ documented at least 78 assaults against journalists from August 2012 until Morsi's fall from power in July 2013. Muslim Brotherhood supporters were responsible for 72 of the attacks, CPJ found, with a handful of other assaults committed by opposition groups against journalists perceived to be aligned with the Muslim Brotherhood.

The situation turned abruptly against Morsi's supporters after his ouster by the Egyptian military, which closed or heavily censored pro-Morsi news outlets. Foreign news organizations seen as unsympathetic to the military regime, including CNN and Al-Jazeera, were systematically harassed. Since the military took control, at least five journalists were killed, 30 assaulted, and 11 news outlets raided. CPJ has documented the detention of at least 44 journalists. At least five journalists remained behind bars in late 2013.

The government's grip on all media tightened with the imposition of a nationwide state of emergency. Journalists who deviate from the official narrative are in danger of censorship, arrest, prosecution, or assault. There's a sense among reporters that while Morsi's efforts to intimidate the press into silence largely failed, military censorship is starting to take root. "There was definitely a barrier of fear that was broken around January 2011, and I have to say it has come back," said Lina Attalah, chief editor of *Mada Masr*, harking back to the exhilarating early days following the fall of former President Hosni Mubarak. "There is a feeling that we are not able to practice the journalism we had hoped to after the revolution."

## Russia

As Russia prepares to host the 2014 Winter Olympics, the implementation of a series of draconian laws and the prosecution of government opponents have led to the most oppressive and anti-Western climate since the Cold War.

According to new laws enacted in late 2012, local human rights groups and independent watchdogs that receive funding from abroad are required to register as "foreign agents." Russian journalists fear that they can be persecuted for gathering information from organizations not condoned by the government.

On September 18, British freelance journalist Kieron Bryan and Russian freelance photographer Denis Sinyakov were detained and accused of piracy while covering a Greenpeace protest on a ship in the Pechora Sea. When journalists cover certain actions, "the authorities can treat you not as a journalist but as an activist, and this is a new reality," said Elena Milashina, CPJ's Moscow correspondent. "If they can do this to foreigners, imagine what they can do with local journalists." The government has also meddled with reporters covering the upcoming Olympic Games. Authorities "actually came to every journalist I talked to (in Sochi), and they showed the limits of what they could cover and made the journalists feel those limits," said Milashina, who writes for the independent newspaper *Novaya Gazeta*.

Two Russian journalists, Akhmednabi Akhmednabiyev and Mikhail Beketov, died as a result of their work in 2013. No one has been arrested in connection with their deaths. Unsolved journalist murders continue to pile up, exacerbating the climate of fear. In at least 32 such cases, no killer or instigator has been brought to justice, according to CPJ research.

## Syria

The already perilous conditions for journalists in Syria worsened in 2013. For the second year in a row, Syria witnessed the most cases of journalists killed, with at least 18 deaths as of late in the year. In addition, at least 30 journalists were still unaccounted for in Syria, according to CPJ research.

A sharp decline in security conditions has made it virtually impossible for foreign journalists to work in Syria. International news organizations increasingly rely on freelancers. The Rory Peck Trust, a group dedicated to the safety of freelancers, released a statement in August urging journalists to reconsider going to Syria. "This is a new situation where no amount of planning or preparation can reliably reduce the possibility of kidnappings or abduction," the group said.

Dozens of journalists have been abducted by various sides in the conflict, including government forces and pro-government militias; rebel or rebel-affiliated groups; and non-Syrian Islamic extremist groups. Among the rebel groups, the kidnapping of journalists for money or the exchange of prisoners has become increasingly common. In government-controlled territories, foreign journalists continue to be detained and for longer periods of time. Local journalists working without permission are promptly detained or disappear. "Citizen journalism has been demolished inside government-controlled areas in terms of security," said Rami Jarrah, an exiled Syrian blogger and activist. Several journalists were being held by the Assad government in late 2013.

Those who do manage to practice journalism in Syria are heavily censored by whichever faction controls the territory. "You can be a journalist in any part of the country but you have to be part of an agreement and you have to follow the narrative that they want," Jarrah said. "If you are an independent journalist, you are in danger wherever you are."

## Vietnam

Vietnam's crackdown on independent bloggers that began in 2008 intensified in 2013. In Asia, Vietnam is second only to China for the number of journalists jailed, according to CPJ's annual prison census. Among the reporters being held is Nguyen Van Hai, known in Vietnam's blogosphere as Dieu Cay, a blogger imprisoned since

2008. He is a recipient of CPJ's 2013 International Press Freedom Award.

In January, five bloggers who contributed regularly to the Catholic Church's *Vietnam Redemptorist News* were sentenced to harsh jail terms and follow-up periods of house arrest for various antistate crimes. At mid-year, three prominent bloggers, Dinh Nhat Uy, Pham Viet Dao, and Truong Duy Nhat, were detained because their blogging activities had "abused democratic freedoms." After a one-day trial, Uy was sentenced in October to a 15-month suspended prison sentence and one year of house arrest. The other two bloggers were still being held without formal charge in late 2013. Blogger Nguyen Hoang Vi was beaten, stripped, and forced to undergo a vaginal cavity search by state nurses while in custody at Nguyen Cu Trinh Ward in Ho Chi Minh City. Critical blogger Le Anh Hung was arrested and committed to a psychiatric institution against his will.

As Vietnam lacks any privately run media, the blogosphere is the only space for critical reporting. The government's efforts to shut it down were reflected in a decree enacted on September 1, 2013, that specifically targets bloggers and social media users. Among other provisions, Decree 72 on the Management, Provision, and Use of Internet Services and Online Information bans Vietnamese Internet users from linking to or reposting news from international media outlets and restricts the types of content that foreign companies are allowed to host on their Vietnam-related websites or platforms. "Naturally we all fear being thrown into jail. And this is the challenge that each and every blogger in Vietnam has to face not only on a daily basis, but hourly," the editorial team of the collective news blog *Danlambao* (Citizen Journalist), whose members work in anonymity, said in an email statement provided to CPJ. "This is the containment method which is used to stop bloggers' networks from flourishing and expanding."

## Turkey

Turkey in 2013 remained one of the world's leading jailers of journalists. The country continues to promote self-censorship through the widespread use of detentions and criminal prosecutions of journalists. June's anti-government rallies, commonly known as the Gezi Park protests, were accompanied by a crackdown on media outlets in retaliation for independent or pro-opposition coverage.

CPJ documented numerous attacks on local and international journalists as well as obstruction and detention during the protests in Istanbul, Ankara, and elsewhere in Turkey. The Turkish state media regulator, RTÜK, fined four television stations for their coverage of the demonstrations. Prime Minister Recep Tayyip Erdoğan publicly accused the international media of biased coverage, singling out CNN International, the BBC, and Reuters.

Numerous critical columnists, editors, and reporters were fired or forced to resign in apparent retaliation for their coverage of the Gezi Park protests. According to the Turkish Union of Journalists, at least 22 journalists were fired and another 37 were forced to quit, reflecting the fact that Turkish conglomerates own media outlets and are beholden to the government for the welfare of their other business. "Our problem was imprisonment of journalists. Now our problem is whether or not we will be able to do journalism in the first place, because the ones that have remained in media can't really do proper reporting, and the ones that were pushed out of media cannot find work," said a Turkish newspaper journalist who asked for her name to be withheld for fear of reprisal.

Turkey also continues to use broad anti-terror laws to criminalize critical expression and suppress the Kurdish media as well as leftist and nationalist groups. In January, Turkey arrested 11 more journalists on the charge of belonging to a banned terrorist organization.

In August, a court hearing the Ergenekon case—an alleged broad anti-government conspiracy—declared at least 20 journalists guilty of involvement in the plot and doled out lengthy prison sentences. However, most journalists imprisoned in Turkey were kept in pretrial detention, and many had not seen the indictments against them.

## Bangladesh

Street clashes between Islamists and secularists led to a rapidly deteriorating press freedom climate in Bangladesh, where journalists speaking out on sensitive issues were targeted by all sides. Bloggers increasingly became the victims of violence and government persecution. Blogger Asif Mohiuddin was stabbed in January as he left his office in Dhaka. The following month, another blogger, Ahmed Rajib Haider, was killed for his writing.

An ongoing war crimes tribunal prosecuting genocide, crimes against humanity, and other crimes dating back to the 1971 war of independence from Pakistan inflamed tensions and led to a series of protests across the country. The sentencing of a senior Islamist leader with a life term in February set off nationwide demonstrations known as the "Shahbagh movement," in which protesters called for the death penalty. Four secular bloggers were arrested in April for allegedly inciting religious tension, and their blogs were shut down. Islamists responded with their own mass protests calling for the bloggers to be put to death. Journalists who have covered the Shahbagh and Islamist protests were harassed and physically attacked. Ekushey Television reporter Nadia Sharmeen was beaten by a crowd while covering an Islamist protest in April.

Mahmudur Rahman, editor of the pro-opposition newspaper *Amar Desh*, was imprisoned on charges of publishing false and derogatory information and sedition. The Awami League–controlled government also halted the broadcasts of four opposition channels. "There is a lot of misunderstanding in this society," said Mainul Islam Khan, co-director of the press freedom group the Bangladesh Centre for Development, Journalism, and Communication. "If you don't let the other side speak, it creates tension," he said.

## Liberia

President Ellen Johnson Sirleaf's administration promised more open and democratic rule in Liberia after years of civil war and dictatorship. The past year, however, has seen a climate of self-censorship take hold. Worrisome developments include the jailing of journalists in civil libel cases and bankrupting of their news organizations by imposing exorbitant damages.

More than a year after signing the Declaration of Table Mountain—a call for the repeal of criminal defamation and "insult" laws across Africa—Sirleaf's administration has done little to advance the cause of decriminalizing defamation. In addition, civil cases brought by government officials have resulted in excessive financial damage awards. In August, a ruling imposing a US$1.5 million fine forced the closure of the leading independent newspaper, *FrontPageAfrica*, and the imprisonment of its managing editor and publisher, Rodney Sieh, in a case tainted with political undertones. Sieh was jailed indefinitely pending payment, then released on temporary "compassionate leave." In November, a court formally closed the proceedings against Sieh and *FrontPageAfrica* after the libel claims were dropped amid an international outcry.

*FrontPageAfrica* has repeatedly reported on corruption, official misconduct, and human rights abuses, and local journalists told CPJ that the heavy fine was a clear ploy to shut down the critical newspaper. No newspaper has won a libel case since Sirleaf's election in 2005, according to the Press Union of Liberia. "When officials of government are so keen to run to the courts with issues like these, that are in the public interest, it makes it more difficult for the press to work freely," said Peter Quaqua, president of the union.

Adding to the tense environment for journalists, a key Sirleaf aide set off a firestorm with an inflammatory speech on World Press Freedom Day. Othello Daniel Warrick, President Sirleaf's chief security aide, referred to journalists as "terrorists," and said he would "go after" any journalist who publishes articles critical of the presidency.

## Ecuador

While defamation suits and public insults by officials continue to be used to intimidate the press in Ecuador, a new series of legal measures enacted by President Rafael Correa's administration further degraded the press freedom climate in 2013.

The new Communications Law, approved in June by the Ecuadoran National Assembly to regulate editorial content, gives authorities the power to impose arbitrary sanctions and censor the press. The law mandates a state watchdog to monitor media content, and is filled with ambiguous language demanding that journalists provide accurate and balanced information or face civil or criminal penalties. The recently named superintendent of communication and information, Carlos Ochoa, is known for publicly insulting the press. "The atmosphere is much worse because of the law," said Monica Almeida, editor at newspaper *El Universo*. "Before, there was a level of control by the government . . . but they did not have this legal framework like the Communications Law which allows them to do many things in their favor."

Earlier in the year, new legislation barring the news media from promoting political candidates "directly or indirectly" in the 90 days before an election led to broad self-censorship among the Ecuadorian media. The law was widely regarded as a way to stifle criticism of Correa in his bid for re-election on February 17, and resulted in scant, shallow reporting on election issues in the press. "There was a serious lack of coverage . . . it was very difficult to do more in-depth work," said Almeida.

## Zambia

In September 2011, after two decades of one-party rule in Zambia, the Patriotic Front government led by President Michael Sata promised an era of greater media freedom. Now, however, the mostly state-owned press is under more pressure to self-censor than ever, while the small space that started to open for independent journalists is shrinking.

Zambian leaders have long invoked criminal defamation laws to intimidate journalists, and Sata has been quick to use them, according to freelance journalist Paul Carlucci. The government pursued independent journalists with a series of vague and spurious charges. Authorities accused Zambian journalist Wilson Pondamali, suspected of being linked to the blocked news website *Zambian Watchdog*, with sedition and insulting the president—charges that eventually shifted to theft of a library book and being in possession of military stores. Two other journalists suspected of links to the *Zambian Watchdog*, Thomas Zyambo and former journalism lecturer Clayson Hamasaka, also faced a variety of charges, ranging from drug possession to insulting the president, which have shifted as police investigations have evolved. "I am heavily restricted in my movements . . . I don't know what they are trying to achieve, other than intimidation," Hamasaka said. "All of my colleagues are scared. Right now, if you do dare any critical reporting, you will be arrested."

*Zambia Reports*, a news website launched in February 2012, was blocked in July. The managing editor told CPJ that the staff believed the government was responsible. *Zambia Reports* filed a complaint with the Zambian Information & Communication Technology Authority (ZICTA) on July 22, but received no reply.

**Maya Taal** *is a freelance writer based in Brussels. She previously worked in communications for CPJ and for Human Rights Watch.*

# Index